TEACHER RESOURCES FOR A HOME IN THE WILDERNESS

2024 Edition

Amanda M. Cetas & Adriana R. King

Windy Sea Publishing, LLC | Tucson, Arizona

Teacher Resources for A Home in the Wilderness

Windy Sea Publishing
Tucson, AZ
www.windyseapublishing.com

Copyright © 2024 First Edition
Windy Sea Publishing

ISBN-13: 978-1-956277-17-3

Cover Design: A. Marie Hanson

Jacket Images:
Map: *New Netherlands Map* published by Nicolaes Visscher ** (1649-1702), Public Domain
Novel cover design by Katherine Nskvsky

Table of Contents

About the Authors

Amanda M. Cetas is the author of the historical adventure *A Home in the Wilderness*, which is the second book in the series, *A Country for Castoffs*. The story is taken from her family history, which she has spent over two decades researching. She is recently retired from teaching several courses in American, European and World history to middle grade and advanced high school students. She also taught government and economics courses to high school students during the last few years.

Adriana R. King has been passionate about the art of story telling her whole life, but it wasn't until college in NYC that she discovered the depth and beauty of a story well-told. She also studied abroad at Oxford University. There she learned that every literary technique carries its own value in a story. After college, she spent 3 years as an English teacher where she provided individualized writing feedback and discovered that editing makes our minds stronger and our writing more intentional.

Note to Teachers

There are many resources available covering the early North American colonies at Jamestown and Plymouth, but little for the lesser-known Dutch colony of New Netherlands. The early colonial period is important in establishing the foundational principals of the United States and for developing the spirit of independence in these new Americans.

In creating this guide, we hope to provide a different perspective on the reasons for European emigration and the resulting interactions between these newly arrived European colonists and the existing Native American tribes. Many of the themes will be familiar. In examining this period through a different lens, we hope to broaden students understanding of the complexities of this period by examining new perspectives and contributions by both European and Native participants.

This guide is designed to provide teachers with resources they can use to help their students understand this period through engaging activities, varied learning opportunities, and utilizes both formative and summative assessment methods. Suggestions are provided about how to adapt these resources to your classroom. The resources provided here were developed from years of experience in teaching and educational research on student-centered instruction.

Adjusting for Students with Differing Abilities

Teachers of students at all levels – from middle school to high school – can use these materials successfully. Some of the materials have already been scaffolded, such as some of the historical summaries. Teachers can also use the materials in different ways or adjust them to address their own teaching style and the needs of their students.

Here are some suggestions:

- Use the Bell Ringers to introduce the topics discussed in each section of the reading.

- Read some sections of the readings out loud.

- Break up the readings into shorter chunks.

- Preview the vocabulary and key concepts listed in the Concept Maps. Establish a system to help students find the definitions and use the words in context.

- Use images to associate with difficult or unfamiliar vocabulary words.

- The discussion questions can be done individually by students or in small groups. They can be written or discussed orally or written and then discussed either in small groups or in large class discussions. It has been shown that giving students a chance to read and answer questions, and then to discuss their answers in small groups, before sharing with the class, can help to build student confidence in class discussions/activities.

- The projects and simulations also provide opportunities to group students in different ways and provide opportunities for students to demonstrate their knowledge in different ways to highlight their unique strengths and abilities while holding everyone in the group responsible for their contributions.

- Create a Know/Want to Know/Learned (K-W-L) worksheet for students to record what they already know about the early American colonization and what they would like to learn about it. Then as they read, have them complete the "learned" section of the worksheet.

- Brainstorm students' current knowledge and create a class web or graphic organizer to connect their ideas about the topics.

- Ask students to complete their own graphic organizers for sections of the reading individually or in pairs.

Assessing Student Achievement

Numerous tools for assessing, including rubrics, are available throughout this guide and in Appendix A.

Grading Group Assignments: Group work can be motivating for students, but it can also be a source of conflict. To mitigate some of this conflict, keep groups small, ideally no more than three to four students to a group. Each student should have their own area of responsibility. For larger classes, five in a group can work, but it is even more important to have designated assignments, that are known to everyone in the group and the teacher. It can also be helpful to have students within the group assess the effectiveness of their group, as well as their own performance, at the end.

Testing: The activities in this resource have been designed to teach students to think critically, analyze multiple perspectives, and articulate individual conclusions. Essay prompts have been provided to help students demonstrate critical thinking and historical understanding. These can also be modified into short answer responses depending on student abilities. In some cases, teachers may opt to provide a single prompt or assessment to the class, or the teacher may choose to provide several choices from which students may select from a list of prompts or assessments.

Cross-Curricular Opportunities

While the bulk of the methods in this resource are designed for English Language Arts and history courses, some of the activities, projects, and simulations tie to economics and science and can be integrated into a variety of courses or used effectively in a cross-curricular program.

Literature: This unit provides opportunities to explore narrative in historical fiction and to compare it to informational texts. Additionally, several lessons teach an understanding of various literary elements such as, symbolism, foreshadowing, and narrative perspectives/voices. Lessons explore the purpose of myths and compare different cultural traditions. Various assessments allow students to practice writing informative, analytical, comparative, argumentative, and narrative essays.

Social Studies: This unit provides historical background information on the Dutch colony of New Netherlands and the Lenape tribe. Additionally, a research project is provided in which students are asked to study different Native American cultures to evaluate their findings and make comparisons between them. Then students will learn about the Esopus Wars and compare them to other colonial wars between English colonists and other Native American tribes. Students will study the peace treaty process between colonists and native peoples and will learn to analyze primary sources by examining the peace treaties and comparing the "Journal of the Second Esopus War by Capt. Martin Kregier" to secondary retellings. There is also a lesson comparing different cultural understanding of time and a timeline of the development of clocks with accompanying questions to develop higher order thinking skills.

STEM: This unit provides opportunities to learn the economic benefit of trade through an interactive trade simulation. The sundial project provides the opportunity to incorporate a science experiment in which students will create a sundial and test how the position of the sun effects the shadow formed on the sundial at different times of the year.

El Caracol Mayan Observatory, Chichen Itza, Yucantan peninsula, Mexico
Photo by Mariordo (Mario Roberto Durán Ortiz, March 9, 2011
Creative Commons Attribution only license CC BY 4.0
http://creativecommons.org/licenses/by/4.0/

Concept Map

Concept Map of *A Home in the Wilderness*: Part 1: Preparation

Etienne is faced with a difficult choice: Does he stay home and help to defend his community from an impending attack from a neighboring Native American tribe, or does he go in search of his Lenape friends who might be in danger from angry colonists?

KEY LEARNING(S)	UNIT ESSENTIAL QUESTIONS		OPTIONAL INSTRUCTION TOOLS
PICTURE ANALYSIS	**PART 1 HISTORICAL SUMMARY**	**PROLOGUE & CHAPTER 1**	**CHAPTERS 2-3**
Landing of Henry Hudson, *1609, at Verplanck Point, New York* Robert Walter Weir (1803-1899)	History of the Dutch colony of New Netherlands Purchase of Manhattan History of the Lenape tribe	Etienne is late for a double-wedding and learns of the attack on Wiltwyck. Now his Lenape friends may be in danger.	As New Harlem prepares its defenses, Etienne must choose which side of the conflict to support.
ESSENTIAL QUESTIONS	**ESSENTIAL QUESTIONS**	**ESSENTIAL QUESTIONS**	**ESSENTIAL QUESTIONS**
1. Describe the body postures of the Dutch. Based on what you see, what do you think they want to say to the Native Americans? What do they want? 2. Describe the body postures of the Native Americans. Based on the clues you see in the image. what do you think they want to say to the Dutch? What do you think their response will be? 3. Does this meeting of the two different groups people appear to be friendly or hostile? Why? Explain your answer.	1. What is the primary purpose of this text (informative, persuasive/argumentative, entertaining)? Does the author(s) reveal his/her bias (opinion) about the Dutch or the Native Americans? If so, what is their bias, and how do you know? If not, how did they maintain a neutral tone? 2. Based on the information in the text, what were the two reasons the Dutch came to the region of North America that became New Netherlands? 3. In your own words, describe the three factors that must be considered in judging the fairness of the Dutch purchase of Manhattan. 4. Explain why Native American societies would be organized based on gender roles.	1. What symbolic meaning(s) might the fire represent in the prologue? 2. What significance do wampum belts have in Alsoomse's society? What does this tell us about their societies? 3. The first paragraph serves as foreshadowing for the rest of the book. How does the author use this technique to draw readers into the story? 4. What details does the author provide in the text and what do they tell the reader about the narrator's personality, and other physical, mental, or emotional characteristics? 5. How does the setting (time and place) of this story relate to the historical summary? Where and when in the series of events listed in the historical summary does this story fit in?	1. Based on what you read, did the settlers in New Harlem have a legitimate fear of a possible attack by native tribes? Why or why not? 2. From the clues given in the chapter, what can you infer about the relationships between the Dutch settlers in Wiltwyck and the native tribes in the area? Why do you think the Esopus attacked the settlement of Wiltwyck? 3. What reasons did Mr. Gayneau give for not wanting to fight? What was he willing to do for his community? Do you think Etienne's father was a coward? Why or why not? 4. Why didn't the settlers go to war immediately? What two things did they do first? What does that imply about their life on Manhattan prior to the attack on Wiltwyck?
VOCABULARY	**VOCABULARY**	**VOCABULARY**	**VOCABULARY**
	With Annotation Guide – Use the annotation guide to identify unknown or important words. Without Annotation Guide - Underline all the words that appear to be technical history terms (Scaffolded: Use the highlighted words). Use the context around the word to create a guess definition then look up the word in the dictionary.	Wampum Sanctuary Procession Demeanor Cacophony Satchel Militia Migtate	Calloused Schout Hysteria Infiltrate Coalition Immorality Demolishing Vulnerable Chastise
COMMON CORE STANDARDS	**COMMON CORE STANDARDS**	**COMMON CORE STANDARDS**	**COMMON CORE STANDARDS**
	CCSS.ELA-LITERACY.RI.8.1-8	CCSS.ELA-Literacy.RL.8.1-7, 9; L.8.1-5	CCSS.ELA-Literacy.RL.8.1-7, 9; L.8.1-5

ADDITIONAL INFORMATION

4

Concept Map of *A Home in the Wilderness*: Part 1: Preparation

Etienne is faced with a difficult choice: Does he stay home and help to defend his community from an impending attack from a neighboring Native American tribe, or does he go in search of his Lenape friends who might be in danger from angry colonists?

KEY LEARNING(S)	UNIT ESSENTIAL QUESTIONS		OPTIONAL INSTRUCTION TOOLS
CHAPTER 4	**CHAPTER 5**	**CHAPTER 6**	**CHAPTER 7**
Etienne must make a hard decision and only time will tell if it was the right one.	Etienne heads out into the forest to search for his Lenape friends and encounters challenges along the way.	Etienne and his friends head north to help with the negotiations to return prisoners.	Alsoomse and her brothers witness Etienne being captured and follow, waiting for their opportunity to free him.
ESSENTIAL QUESTIONS	**ESSENTIAL QUESTIONS**	**ESSENTIAL QUESTIONS**	**ESSENTIAL QUESTIONS**
1. What skills did Etienne learn from his Lenape friends? Why were those important lessons? How would they help him in the new world? 2. What natural resources did the Lenape use in making tools, weapons, and means of transportation? 3. The colonists had their own rowboats. Why would they value the native-made canoes so highly? Have you ever been in a rowboat or a canoe or kayak? If so, consider the differences between these types of boats in terms of maneuverability, stability, and ease of use.	1. What roles do stories and myths serve in communities? 2. In Lenape culture, animals represented different traits and skills. What was a spirit animal? Why would it have been important for boys becoming men to find their spirit animal? What other important skills did boys have to demonstrate in their coming-of-age ceremonies? 3. The wolf and the eagle are used symbolically throughout this book. What might Etienne's confrontation with the wolf mean? 4. How did the methods of negotiating peace differ between the Dutch and Lenape people? How could these differences lead to misunderstandings?	1. What is foreshadowing? How does this technique add to the suspense of the story? 2. How does the author make use of symbolism in this passage? 3. Is pacifism the same as cowardice? Is there ever a time to fight, or should war be avoided at all costs? 4. Why are gender-based roles so common in societies? 5. Why do you think people so often mistreat others the very same way they have been mistreated?	1. Evaluate Hassun's objections to Kitchi's plan of scaling the palisades? Are they valid; in other words, do they have merit? Why do you think Hassun is willing to follow his younger brother's suggestions? What abilities does Kitchi bring to this rescue operation? What skills and experiences does Hassun have? What strengths does Alsoomse have? 2. The willow tree is often given human characteristics in this story. This is called anthropomorphism. Etienne also interacted with a willow tree in chapter 3. Based on these two scenes, what purpose does the willow tree serve in this story? What does it represent or symbolize?
VOCABULARY	**VOCABULARY**	**VOCABULARY**	**VOCABULARY**
Stockade Precaution Voracious Scrutiny Counterbalance Maneuver Torrent Betrothed	Outcropping Meager Bargain Meander Sufficient Compromise Smudge Wigwam Claustrophobia	Pacifist Reverie Incapable Abducted Malicious Interpreter Barracks	Distraction Confrontation Subsequent Palisade
COMMON CORE STANDARDS	**COMMON CORE STANDARDS**	**COMMON CORE STANDARDS**	**COMMON CORE STANDARDS**
CCSS.ELA-Literacy.RL.8.1-7, 9; L.8.1-5	CCSS.ELA-Literacy.RL.8.1-7, 9; L.8.1-5	CCSS.ELA-Literacy.RL.8.1-7, 9; L.8.1-5	CCSS.ELA-Literacy.RL.8.1-7, 9; L.8.1-5

ADDITIONAL INFORMATION

Concept Map of *A Home in the Wilderness*: Part 1: Preparation

Etienne is faced with a difficult choice: Does he stay home and help to defend his community from an impending attack from a neighboring Native American tribe, or does he go in search of his Lenape friends who might be in danger from angry colonists?

KEY LEARNING(S)	UNIT ESSENTIAL QUESTIONS	OPTIONAL INSTRUCTION TOOLS	
CHAPTER 8	**TRADE SIMULATION**	**CONTINUITY & CHANGE OVER TIME ESSAY**	**RESEARCH PROJECT**
Etienne is taken prisoner and is held in Fort Wiltwyck.	Students will take on the roles of Native Americans and colonists, assess their respective economic strengths and weaknesses, evaluate their trade options, and assess whether trade will benefit them.		Research selected Native American tribes from the Southeast, Great Plains, Southwest, Great Basis, NW Coast, Plateau, and California regions and compare their socioeconomic, cultural, and political characteristics.
ESSENTIAL QUESTIONS	**ESSENTIAL QUESTIONS**	**ESSAY PROMPT**	**LEARNING OBJECTIVES**
1. Does Etienne learn any useful information in this chapter? Explain. 2. One of the soldiers mentions that the War Council had approved the commander's ruling prohibiting soldiers from drinking alcohol. Why do you think the commander would make this ordinance? 3. What rules are you required to follow, either at home, school, clubs, sports, or other organizations. Why do you think those rules are there? What purpose do they serve?	1. What resources are you good at producing? What are you inefficient at producing? 2. What resources do you need to survive the winter? What resources do you have? 3. Can you survive the winter with what you have? 4. If you could improve your situation, what would you improve? 5. What could trade to improve your lifestyle? 6. What does the other group do better than their own group? 7. If they could make a trade with the other group, would they be able to improve their lifestyle? 8. How did trading with the other group benefit your group? 9. What must be true for two groups to want to make a trade?	After completing the Trade Simulation, write an essay describing the continuities and change over time for your assigned societies lifestyle resulting from trade. Consider their lifestyle before and after trade networks were established. Also, explain how trade networks were established. Support your answer with specific evidence. Finally, make a conclusion stating your opinion on whether your society was better off before or after trading and why.	1. Understand the social and economic characteristics of various Native American tribes. 2. Understand the cultural/religious characteristics of those tribes. 3. Understand the political and geographical characteristics of the tribes. 4. What conclusions can you make about the way native peoples lived in North America? Essay Prompt: Compare and contrast the characteristics of the different tribal communities. Consider the gender roles, governmental/leadership structures, economies, religious beliefs, and other cultural considerations.
VOCABULARY	**VOCABULARY**	**VOCABULARY**	**VOCABULARY**
Blockhouse			
COMMON CORE STANDARDS	**COMMON CORE STANDARDS**	**COMMON CORE STANDARDS**	**COMMON CORE STANDARDS**
CCSS.ELA-Literacy.RL.8.1-7, 9; L.8.1-5	CCSS.ELA-Literacy.RI.8.1-3, 6; L.8.1-5	CCSS.ELA-Literacy.RL.8.1-7, 9; W.8.2a-f, 4-6; L.8.1-5	CCSS.ELA-Literacy. W.8.2a-f, 7-9a-b; SL.8.1a-d, 4-6; L.8.1-3

ADDITIONAL INFORMATION

Concept Map of *A Home in the Wilderness*: Part 2: Rescue

Etienne and his friends help to rescue a colonial woman and return her to the fort, before heading off to war.

KEY LEARNING(S)	UNIT ESSENTIAL QUESTIONS		OPTIONAL INSTRUCTION TOOLS
PICTURE ANALYSIS	**PART 2 HISTORICAL SUMMARY**	**CHAPTER 9**	**CHAPTERS 10 & 11**
Painting of Fort Wiltwyck, 1695 Kingston, *by Len Tantillo, 2015*	Earlier Colonial-Native American wars background The Esopus Wars history	Alsoomse and her brothers escape from Fort Wiltwyck, but without Etienne.	The war council at Wiltwyck decides to send Noshi and the Mohawks to negotiate with the Esopus for the return of the captives.
ESSENTIAL QUESTIONS	**ESSENTIAL QUESTIONS**	**ESSENTIAL QUESTIONS**	**ESSENTIAL QUESTIONS**
1. Describe the defensive structures visible in this image. 2. What else do you notice in this image? For example, what can you tell about the layout of the town? What purpose do the structures and fenced areas seem to serve? What types of structures are outside of the town walls? How is the land being used? 3. What can you infer about what life was like living in and around Fort Wiltwyck? Why might some people choose to live outside the fort walls? What might this tell you about their expectations or relationships with surrounding native tribes?	1. What resulted from each conflict? Which side won? What happened to the losing side? What factors explain these results? 2. How did these conflicts impact the areas where they were fought? In other words, considering what life was like in these regions before the conflicts and what it was like after the conflicts, why are these conflicts considered to be "turning points in history"?	1. What method does the author use to distinguish Alsoomse's chapters from those told by Etienne? 2. How does the author's use of different narrative styles change the relationship the reader has with the characters, or does it? 3. Why do you think the author uses this technique when shifting character perspectives? Do you think it is effective? Why or why not? 4. How does Hassun feel about Etienne? What actions or events might have caused him to feel this way? Is he justified in feeling this way? Why or why not? Do you think he is treating Etienne fairly? Why or why not?	1. Why did the Dutch let Noshi, the Mohawks and Etienne go? What were they supposed to do? 2. What do you think explains the actions of the Dutch when they come to Kanti's village? 3. Why might the Dutch have a difficult time determining which tribes or villages were hostile, friendly, or neutral? 4. How do the different perspectives of this conflict, as seen in the war council meeting and Kanti's retelling compare? How does it broaden your understanding of this conflict?
VOCABULARY	**VOCABULARY**	**VOCABULARY**	**VOCABULARY**
	Underline all the words that appear to be technical history terms (Scaffolded: Use the highlighted words). Use the context around the word to create a guess definition then look up the word in the dictionary.		Sensation Biceps Guilder
COMMON CORE STANDARDS	**COMMON CORE STANDARDS** **CCSS.ELA-LITERACY.**RI.8.1, 5, 6, 7	**COMMON CORE STANDARDS** **CCSS.ELA-Literacy.** RL.8.1-7, 9; L.8.1-5	**COMMON CORE STANDARDS** **CCSS.ELA-Literacy.** RL.8.1-7, 9; L.8.1-5
ADDITIONAL INFORMATION			

Concept Map of *A Home in the Wilderness*: Part 2: Rescue

Etienne and his friends help to rescue a colonial woman and return her to the fort, before heading off to war.

KEY LEARNING(S)	UNIT ESSENTIAL QUESTIONS	OPTIONAL INSTRUCTION TOOLS	
CHAPTER 12	**CHAPTERS 13-14**	**CHAPTERS 15-17**	**CHAPTERS 18-19**
Etienne and his friends rescue a colonial woman from the Esopus.	Reinforcements arrive and the Dutch army organizes to go out and fight the Esopus.	Etienne rescues a boy and girl from the fire and is captured.	Etienne escapes and his friends come to his rescue as he is chased through the forest.

ESSENTIAL QUESTIONS	ESSENTIAL QUESTIONS	ESSENTIAL QUESTIONS	ESSENTIAL QUESTIONS
1. Compare the two creation stories. Why might they be so similar? What might explain their differences? 2. How did evil enter the world according to Alsoomse's story? How did evil enter the world according to the Algonquian story? Who is to blame for evil entering the world in each story? How might these differences affect or influence the religious practices or beliefs of each society?	1. What different attitudes about the colonists and Native Americans did you see expressed? Why do you think there were so many different opinions? Did each opinion have valid points? Where did they go too far or fail to consider the other groups perspectives? 2. Based on your conclusions, how do you think we can do a better job of solving our conflicts today?	1. In what ways did Etienne react impulsively in these chapters? What impact did his actions have on other people? How did his actions affect himself? What, if anything, should he have done differently? What, if anything, did he do right? 2. Are impulses good or bad? How to past experiences shape our impulses?	1. How does Kitchi's character change throughout this story? What clues does the author give to show the reader how he has grown up? 2. How has Alsoomse changed from the beginning of the story? How has her relationship with her father and brothers changed? Her father used to tolerate her willfulness. How has he reacted to her recent rebelliousness? What might explain this change?

VOCABULARY	VOCABULARY	VOCABULARY	VOCABULARY
Manito Sinister Solitary Acknowledgment	Leverage Agitated Sachem Meager Garrison Commandeered Unanimously Suspicious Inarticulate Remnants	Impulse Pandemonium Embolden Betrayal Unconsciousness	Careen Unwavering Menace Ambush Hypocrisy

COMMON CORE STANDARDS	COMMON CORE STANDARDS	COMMON CORE STANDARDS	COMMON CORE STANDARDS
CCSS.ELA-Literacy.RL.8.1-7, 9; L.8.1-5	CCSS.ELA-Literacy.RL.8.1-7, 9; L.8.1-5	CCSS.ELA-Literacy.RL.8.1-7, 9; L.8.1-5	CCSS.ELA-Literacy.RL.8.1-7, 9; L.8.1-5

ADDITIONAL INFORMATION

Chapter 12: Will need a copy of Genesis 1-3. Free copies may be accessed at https://www.biblegateway.com.

8

Concept Map of *A Home in the Wilderness*: Part 2: Rescue

Etienne and his friends help to rescue a colonial woman and return her to the fort, before heading off to war.

KEY LEARNING(S)	UNIT ESSENTIAL QUESTIONS	OPTIONAL INSTRUCTION TOOLS	
CHAPTERS 20-21	**ESSAY/CREATIVE WRITING**	**COMPARING PRIMARY SOURCES TO HISTORICAL RETELLINGS**	**ANALYTICAL ESSAY**
Etienne and his friends return to New Harlem and form a plan for continued peace with the Dutch colonists.		Students will compare the events as they are told in the Journal to the author's retelling in chapters part 2 of *A Home in the Wilderness*.	
ESSENTIAL QUESTIONS	**ESSAY PROMPT**	**LEARNING OBJECTIVES**	**Essay Prompt**
1. What purpose do myths serve? Why did the author choose to include this one in the chapter? 2. Why does Etienne's father decide to leave the sachem and his warriors in his house and go to bring the leaders of New Harlem back with him, rather than simply taking the Native Americans to the town council? 3. What information what exchanged in the meeting? What concessions did each party ask for? How did the colonists and the Lenape seal the deal they made? What items and/or promises were exchanged?	Cultures around the world created myths to explain how the world came into existence, how man was created, or other realities of their world. Create your own myth to explain how something, perhaps an animal, a place, or a community, came to be.	1. Compare the Journal to the information given in the novel. What details or facts did the author include? What facts or details did she leave out? 2. How accurate do you think the author's retelling of these events is? Explain your answer. 3. Which version of the events, the primary source or the retelling, is more interesting to read? Which version made a greater impact on you? Why? 4. What is the purpose of each document? Who are their intended audiences?	How does purpose and audience affect the writing style, type of information and details included in a historical document compared to a work of historical fiction?
VOCABULARY	**VOCABULARY**	**VOCABULARY**	**VOCABULARY**
Memento Staccato Abduct Permeating Delegation Inadvertently Bill			
COMMON CORE STANDARDS	**COMMON CORE STANDARDS**	**COMMON CORE STANDARDS**	**COMMON CORE STANDARDS**
CCSS.ELA-Literacy.RL.8.1-7, 9; L.8.1-5	CCSS.ELA-Literacy.W.8.3a-e, 4-6; L.8.1-5	CCSS.ELA-Literacy.SL.8.1a-d, 2-6; L.8.1-3	CCSS.ELA-Literacy.W.8.1a-e, 4-6: L.8.1-5

ADDITIONAL INFORMATION

* The "Journal of the Second Esopus War: By Capt. Martin Kregier" is available for download at https://www.amandamcetas.com/supplemental-materials.

Concept Map of *A Home in the Wilderness*: Part 3: Negotiating Peace

Etienne and his Native American friends go to negotiate peace with the Dutch colonists and Etienne looks to the future.

KEY LEARNING(S)		UNIT ESSENTIAL QUESTIONS	OPTIONAL INSTRUCTION TOOLS
PICTURE ANALYSIS	**PRIMARY SOURCE ANALYSIS***	**CHAPTER 22**	**CHAPTERS 23-24**
The Treaty of Pomeiock, *by Spencer Nichols*	This is an activity where students will research and share what they have learned about the peace agreement between the Dutch/English colonists and the Esopus tribes.	Etienne accompanies his father and the Lenape to New Amsterdam for the negotiations.	The Lenape village is attacked and Etienne and his friends rush to help.
ESSENTIAL QUESTIONS	**ESSENTIAL QUESTIONS**	**ESSENTIAL QUESTIONS**	**ESSENTIAL QUESTIONS**
1. Describe what you see in this image in your own words? 2. Based on this image, what inferences can you make about how the people in this community live, their relationships with other groups of people, their relationships within the community? 3. What specific elements of this image support the conclusions you made in the above question?	1. why is it significant, or important, that this treaty was renewed a number of times? 2. What, if anything, surprises you in these documents? What stood out to you as important or interesting?	1. Why do you think Etienne's father wanted to avoid becoming indentured? What would it mean for his family? 2. How does Etienne's father propose to come up with the money the family needs? What plan does Etienne devise? 3. Can you think of any other ways that Etienne and his father could raise the money to pay their debt?	1. What does the fire symbolize in the Prologue? Support your answer with evidence from the text. 2. What other meanings does the fire represent? 3. Where does the author use fire as a foreshadowing of events to come? 4. How does Jean demonstrate his remorse and repentance for his role in the tragedy? 5. What was the makeup of the jury? Why is it important? What legal principal does it represent?
VOCABULARY	**VOCABULARY**	**VOCABULARY**	**VOCABULARY**
		Indentured servitude Nocturnal Ominous Parapet Terminus Amputated Converse	Intuition Intention Skulk Jostling Impotent Pinnacle Incoherent Calamity
COMMON CORE STANDARDS	**COMMON CORE STANDARDS** **CCSS.ELA-LITERACY.RH.8.1-9; SL.8.1a-d, 2,**	**COMMON CORE STANDARDS**	**COMMON CORE STANDARDS** **CCSS.ELA-Literacy.RL.8.1-7, 9; L.8.1-5**

ADDITIONAL INFORMATION

* *An Agreement made between Richard Nicolls Esq., Governor and the Sachems and People called the Sopes Indyans. 7th day of October 1665* at the following link:
https://clerk.ulstercountyny.gov/sites/default/files/resources/Nicolls%20Esopus%20Peace%20Treaty_2015.pdf

10

Concept Map of *A Home in the Wilderness*: Part 3: Negotiating Peace

Etienne and his Native American friends go to negotiate peace with the Dutch colonists and Etienne looks to the future.

KEY LEARNING(S)		UNIT ESSENTIAL QUESTIONS	OPTIONAL INSTRUCTION TOOLS
CHAPTERS 25-27	**CHAPTER 28 & EPILOGUE**	**CONTINUITY & CHANGE OVER TIME ESSAY**	**HISTORICAL BACKGROUND**
Etienne sells his dugout canoe and signs on to work on one of Captain Carteret's ships.	Alsoomse witnesses the peace agreement with the Esopus.	Using information from the novel, your research on Native American tribes (and notes from other classmates' presentations, if applicable), and any appropriate prior knowledge, answer the following question. Include an arguable thesis statement and be sure to support your answer with specific evidence.	A historical understanding of time: comparing the way different civilizations understood and measured time. The development of clocks timeline.
ESSENTIAL QUESTIONS	**ESSENTIAL QUESTIONS**	**ESSAY PROMPT**	**ESSENTIAL QUESTIONS**
1. Dugout canoes were known to be very valuable to colonists. Why do you think this was? 2. What made dugout canoes more desirable than the plank wood rowboats the colonists made?	1. How has Alsoomse's character grown or evolved throughout this story? 2. How does Noshi's behaviors toward his daughter change? What might explain the change? 3. How do Alsoomse's non-traditional talents aid her tribe in chapter 23? Do you think this will change how her mother sees her? Why or why not? 4. What method does the author use in the epilogue to introduce a new character? Do you think it is effective? Why or why not?	How had relationships among and between Native American tribes changed and stayed the same in terms of culture, economic, political, or social conditions from before Europeans arrive in North America to after various European groups colonized the area.	1. How did the Mayan understanding of time and the creation of their calendar compare with that of the Shang Dynasty in China? How were they different? 2. Why do you think humans have been concerned with measuring time? What purposes does it serve? Did different socio-economic groups have different reasons for wanting to measure time? 3. How do religious beliefs tie in with a civilization's understanding of time?
VOCABULARY	**VOCABULARY**	**VOCABULARY**	
Materialized Florin Derogatory Sympathizer Catechism			
COMMON CORE STANDARDS	**COMMON CORE STANDARDS**	**COMMON CORE STANDARDS**	
CCSS.ELA-Literacy.RL.8.1-7, 9; L.8.1-5	CCSS.ELA-Literacy. RL.8.1-7, 9; L.7.1-5	CCSS.ELA-Literacy. W.8.1a-e, 4-6; L.8.1-3	RH.8.1-7, 9; SL.8.1a-d, 4-6
ADDITIONAL INFORMATION			

Concept Map of *A Home in the Wilderness*: Part 3: Negotiating Peace

Etienne and his Native American friends go to negotiate peace with the Dutch colonists and Etienne looks to the future.

KEY LEARNING(S)	UNIT ESSENTIAL QUESTIONS	OPTIONAL INSTRUCTION TOOLS
Project	**SUMMATIVE ASSESSEMENT**	**WRAP-UP PROJECT**
Students will create a sundial and measure how the movement of the sun can tell us the time of day.	The teacher or students will choose a wrap-up essay from the list provided.	The teacher or the students will choose a wrap-up project from the list provided.

ESSENTIAL QUESTIONS · ESSAY PROMPTS · LEARNING OBJECTIVES

ESSENTIAL QUESTIONS

1. Why does the shadow move throughout the day?

2. Did the length of the shadows stay the same or change? If they changed, how did they change? Why do you think they changed?

ESSAY PROMPTS

1. Why did different groups of European settlers come to North America? What were they hoping to achieve?

2. Based on what you have learned in these lessons, what kinds of relationships did many of European settlers hope to have with the Native American tribes? Were they able to achieve these goals? Why or why not?

3. What kinds of relationships did many of the Native American tribes want to have with the European settlers? Were they able to achieve these goals? Why or why not?

4. Was it inevitable that the European settlers and the Native American tribes would experience conflict between and among the different groups?

5. How do the conflicts between the European colonists and the Native American tribes compare to other conflicts you have studied? In what ways are both conflicts similar? In what ways are they different?

6. Thinking about the conflicts you have studied in this unit and others you have studied, in general terms (big picture), why do different groups of people get into conflicts?

7. As a negotiator it is your job to help the Dutch colonists and the Esopus people resolve their differences peaceably. How would you help them solve this conflict? What would each side have to give up to reach a compromise? What would each side gain from the compromise?

8. Given the destruction that often comes from a total defeat, why is it so difficult for groups of people to agree to compromise? What do you think would have to happen in order for both sides to agree to a compromise?

LEARNING OBJECTIVES

Students will connect the themes in the novel and/or identify crucial scenes, characters, settings, etc. and explain their significance.

VOCABULARY

Gnoman

COMMON CORE STANDARDS	COMMON CORE STANDARDS	COMMON CORE STANDARDS
CCSS.ELA-LITERACY.RST.8.1-4, 7	CCSS.ELA-LITERACY. W.8.1a-e, 4-6; L.8.1-5	CCSS.ELA-Literacy. SL.8.1a-d, 4-6; L.8.1-5

ADDITIONAL INFORMATION

Part 1: Preparations

Objectives:

Interpret visual sources to understand historical context.

Interpret primary and secondary sources.

Compare and contrast primary and secondary sources and analyze the purpose each type of source.

Evaluate the accuracy and usefulness of secondary sources in understanding historical events.

Understand the history of the Dutch colony of New Netherlands and its relationship with other groups of people, both native and colonial.

Understand the economic benefits of trade networks.

Compare and contrast different Native American tribes, in terms of culture, economy, politics, and society.

Handouts:

- *A Home in the Wilderness*, Image 1
- Historical background for part 1 with discussion questions OR annotated historical background for part 1 with discussion questions
- Discussion questions by chapter
- Trade simulation
- Continuity and change over time essay prompt
- Research project
- Comparative essay prompt

Day 1

1. **Bell Ringer:** Students will examine the image in the handout "*A Home in the Wilderness,* Image 1" and answer the questions. Follow up with a discussion of students' answers.

2. Handout to each student a copy of the **"Historical Background for Part 1"** or the **"Annotated Historical Background for Part 1"** and a copy of the **"Discussion Questions"** and tell students that as they read, they

should note any unfamiliar or important words.

   a. <u>With Annotation Guide</u> – Use the annotation guide to identify unknown or important words.

   b. <u>Without Annotation Guide</u> - Underline all the words that appear to be technical history terms (<u>Scaffolded</u>: Use the highlighted words). Use the context around the word to create a guess definition then look up the word in the dictionary.

3. Students should answer the discussion questions after they have finished reading. If time is short, students may be asked to complete the questions for homework.

4. Conduct a class discussion of the questions.

Days 2 - 8

1. As students read each section (one or more chapters) ask them to answer the corresponding **"Discussion Questions."** Students could read the chapters at home or in class. The discussion questions may be given out after the students have completed the reading or ahead of time.

2. Conduct a full class discussion or small group round table discussions of the questions.

Day 9

1. Break students into groups for the trade simulation. Have students read their background information and answer the discussion questions provided in this resource.

2. Conduct a class simulation of a trade scenario.

3. Give students a few minutes to answer the follow up questions before conducting a class discussion of their answers.

4. Use the **"Continuity and Change Over Time Essay Prompt"** as a summative assessment.

Optional Research Project (3-6 days)

1. Individually or in small groups, students will research one Native American tribe from a different area of North America.

2. Students or groups should prepare an exhibit, that could include a diorama, display board, or other creative divice, to assimilate what they have learned about their topic.

3. Students will present their research to the class.

4. Finally, have students answer the comparative essay question.

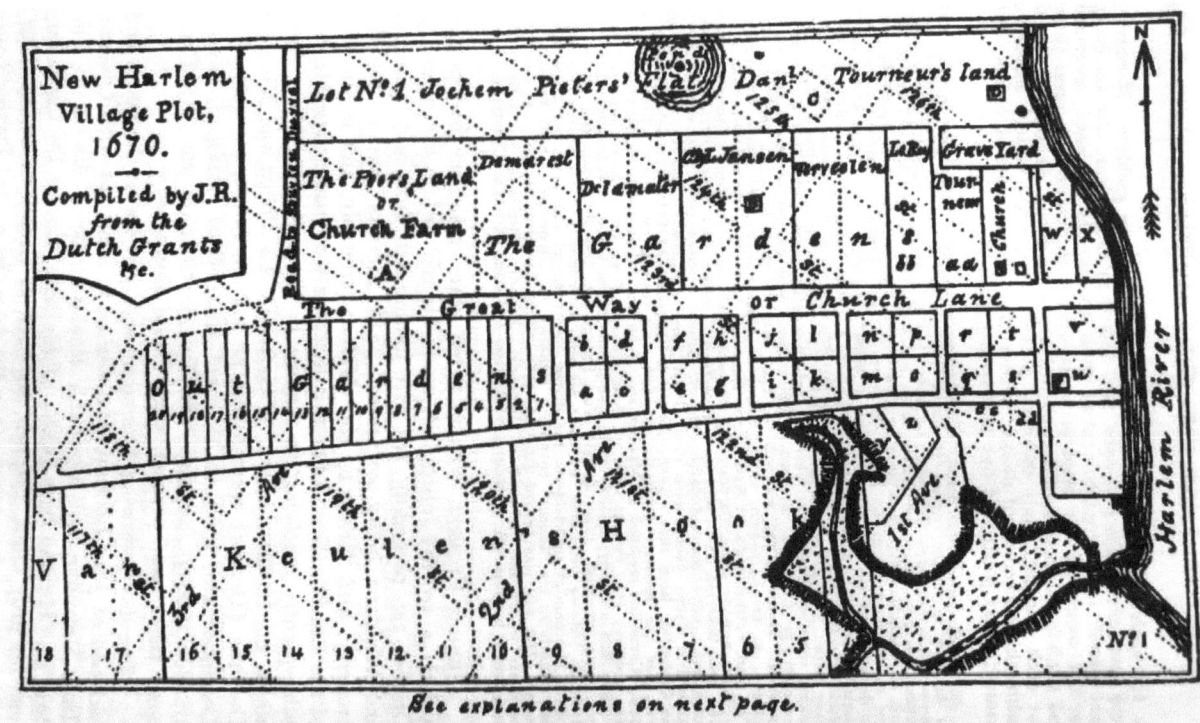

New Harlem Plot Map, 1670, by Ricker James. Public Domain.

Name _____   Class _____   Date _____

A Home in the Wilderness, Image 1

Landing of Henry Hudson, 1609, at Verplanck Point, New York Robert Walter Weir (1803-1899)
Public Domain.

Answer the following questions:

1. Describe the body postures of the Dutch. Based on what you see, what do you think they want to say to the Native Americans? What do they want?

2. Describe the body postures of the Native Americans. Based on the clues you see in the image. what do you think they want to say to the Dutch? What do you think their response will be?

3. Does this meeting of the two different groups people appear to be friendly or hostile? Why? Explain your answer.

Name: _____

Class: _____

Date: _____

Teacher's Section!!

Completeness _____

Comprehension_____

Clarity/Legibility_____

Total Score: _____

Annotation Notes

Historical Background for
A Home in the Wilderness Part 1:
Preparations

1 **History of the Dutch Colony of New**
2 **Netherlands**

3   The Florentine explorer Giovanni da Verrazzano was the first
4 documented European explorer to land on Manhattan in April of
5 1524. He made it to the mouth of the Hudson River before turning
6 back.

7   Manhattan wasn't mapped out until 1609 when Henry
8 Hudson, an English explorer sailing for the Netherlands,
9 arrived and established contact with the Algonquian-
10 speaking Lenape people living there.

11   Hudson's goal was to find a Northwest passage through North
12 America to Asia. Manhattan Island, recorded as *Manna-hata*, in
13 officer Robert Juet's logbook.¹

14   The island's name originates from the Lenape language
15 Munsee, *manaháhtaan* (where *manah-* means "gather", -
16 *aht-* means "bow", and *-aan* is an abstract element used to
17 form verb stems). A reasonable translation of the Lenape word
18 then is "the place for gathering (wood to make) bows." According
19 to research by Albert Seqaqkind Anthony who recorded Munsee
20 traditions, the island was named for the grove of hickory trees that
21 grew on the southern end of the island. The wood from these trees
22 was used to make bows.²

23   The Dutch established a fur trading settlement on
24 Governor's Island in 1624. Two years later, the Dutch
25 purchased the island of Manhattan and began construction
26 of the harbor town of New Amsterdam.

First Impressions
Central Ideas (CI) / Topic
What is the CI/Topic?

_____

_____

_____

Textual Evidence (Use the page and line #s as a reference)

_____

_____

_____

Purpose (POV)
**Circle ONE
A. Entertain
B. Persuade
C. Inform

Textual Evidence (Use the page and line #s as a reference)

_____

_____

_____

_____

¹ Juet, Robert (2006) [1625]. "Juet's Journal of Hudson's 1609 Voyage, from the 1625 Edition of *Purchas His Pilgrimes*". *The New York Times*. Translated by Brea Barthel. p. 16. Archived from the original on July 3, 2016. Retrieved May 11, 2020.

² Goddard, Ives (2010). "The Origin and Meaning of the Name "Manhattan"". *New York History*. **91** (4): 277–293. hdl:10088/16790. ISSN 0146-437X – via Smithsonian Research Online.

16

Name: _____

Coalition War, c. 1625-35. Public Domain.

27
28
29

30 Purchase of Manhattan

31 Popular belief says that the frugal Dutch purchased the
32 island for $24 worth of trinkets and glass beads.[3] However, this
33 legend ignores several important factors.

34 Firstly, it is important to note that the Dutch were foremost
35 traders. They desired peaceable access to trade networks. To that
36 end, they sought a legal transfer of land, rather than a military
37 conquest.

38 Surviving documents from the West India Company indicate
39 that the company authorized the provisional director, Willem
40 Verhulst, to purchase Manhattan.[4] On November 5, 1626 The
41 Hague reported receiving a communication from the colony
42 stating (in translation) that "They have purchased the Island from
43 the *wilden* for the value of 60 guilders."[5]

44 It was a historian in 1846 who first translated the 60
45 guilders into $24, but other scholars have since equated the value
46 in today's currency to varying amounts ranging from $1,000,
47 $2,000, or as much as $15,000.[6]

48 While this might still seem like a steal by today's standards,
49 it should be noted that the Native Americans received tools, iron
50 pots, and other manufactured goods that they were not able to

I Notice

[3] Hsitory.com Editors. *"New Amsterdam becomes New York,"*
History, A&E Television Networks. May 19, 2023. Retrieved March
15, 2024.

[4] Howe, Richard. "Notes On The Manhattan Purchase," The Gotham
Center for New York City History. June 27, 2012. Accessed March
14, 2024.

[5] Janos.NYC, *"Today in NYC History: How the Dutch Actually
Bought Manhattan (The Long Version),"* Today in NYC History. N.d.
Accessed March 14, 2024.

[6] Howe, ibid; Janos.NYC, ibid; Benchley, Nathaniel. *"The $24
Swindle,"* American Heritage Magazine, December 1959. Accessed
March 14, 2024.

Name: _____

Annotation Notes		

Closing Impressions

Central Ideas (CI) / Topic
Has your understanding of the CI/Topic Changed? If so, how? If not, provide an additional piece of textual evidence on the lines below to support your previous CI.

_____

_____

_____

_____

_____

95 lying between the Susquehanna and Delaware rivers, and the
96 southeastern part of New York west of the Hudson River.[11]

97   Archeologists believe the Lenape people inhabited this
98 region for more than five thousand years, long before the arrival
99 of the Europeans, the birth and death of Christ, or even Abraham,
100 the father of the Hebrew and Arab people.[12]

101   Many seventeenth century tribes originated from the Lenape,
102 including the Weckquaesgeek (pronounced phonetically), which
103 lived in the northern part of Manhattan. They were also called
104 Manhattans and Wappingers (by the Dutch).

105   The Weckquaesgeek spoke the Munsee dialect of the
106 Algonquian language and were part of an alliance with the
107 Mohawk in the north.[13]

108   The lower Hudson River area where they lived was very
109 hospitable environment. It was rich in fish, shellfish, game, edible
110 and medicinal plants. The waterways facilitated transportation
111 and trade networks. The land was fertile for planning crops and
112 finding flint, used for arrowheads.[14]

113   They were a peaceful people and largely stayed in one place,
114 migrating only seasonally from the southeastern part of New
115 York to Manhattan to fish and gather the shells used to make
116 wampum. They had largely varied diet consisting of fish,
117 shellfish, game, such as, deer, elk, bear, turkey, snakes, frogs, and
118 beaver, as well as cultivated crops, like corn, squash, and beans,
119 and gathered berries, nuts, and root vegetables. Men did the
120 hunting and fishing, while the women gathered, planted, and
121 harvested the crops.[15]

122   Women were responsible for making all the clothing,
123 adornments, and household goods. They tanned animal pelts for
124 clothing, moccasins, blankets, and coverings for their winter
125 houses, known as *Nash Wetu.* They made clay pottery and used
126 turkey feathers woven together to make lighter weight blankets.
127 They wove reeds into mats to line the inside walls and floors or
128 for making baskets for carrying and storing goods.[16]

129   The men cleared the forest using a slash and burn method of
130 stripping the bark around the base of trees and setting fires
131 around the tree to fell it. Large trees were made into dugout
132 canoes for fishing in Long Island Sound and the Atlantic Ocean.
133 The bark was used for lighter-weight canoes, used for long-
134 distance travel in the calmer rivers. They used bent saplings to
135 make domed bark-covered houses and sleeping platforms along

Textual Evidence to support your CI (Use the page and line #s as a reference)

_____

_____

_____

_____

_____

_____

_____

_____

_____

[11] Alligood, Nekole. "The History of the Delaware Nation,"
Delaware Nation. Web. Accessed 4/9/2024.
[12] Cohen, Doris Darlington. "The Weckquaesgeek." with verbal
guidance from Nicholas Shoumatoff, Curator and Delaware Expert at
Ward Pound Trailside Museum and his library, pg. 1
[13] Alligood, ibid.
[14] Cohen, ibid.
[15] Cohen, ibin.
[16] Cohen, ibin, pgs.5-6.

18

Name: _____

Annotation Notes

136 the inside walls of the homes. They also made lean-tos for
137 summer shade that captured the cooling breezes.[17]

138
139 *The Town of Pomieock*, by Spenser Nicols. Library of Congress
140

141   Men also made weapons and tools from wood, bone, shell
142 and flint rock. They also carved the wampum beads from the
143 oyster shells for use in making jewelry, belts, and trade.[18]

144   The men shaved the sides of their heads with a coxcomb
145 (like the comb of a male rooster), or mohawk, in the front and
146 long hair in the back. They often added feathers or a fox tail
147 hanging down the back.

148   The men plucked their beards and paint their faces in colo[r]
149 of blue, black, yellow, white, or red for ceremonies and warfar[e]
150 They wore beaded necklaces of copper, wampum, shell, and
151 stone.[19]

152   Women had long black hair worn straight or in braids, oft[en]
153 tied with strings or shells. Sometimes they cut bangs across the[ir]
154 foreheads. They wore headbands or small square caps. They wo[re]
155 beaded girdles around their slim waists.[20]

Closing Impressions

Author Bias
Does the author show bias toward any of the people groups mentioned?

_____

_____

_____

_____

_____

Textual Evidence (Use the page and line #s as a reference)

_____

_____

_____

_____

_____

_____

_____

_____

Briefly Summarize the Passage (Use the back or a separate sheet of paper for more space)

---

[17] Cohen, ibin,
[18] Cohen, ibin,, pg. 2
[19] Cohen, ibin, pg. 4
[20] Cohan, ibin,

Name _____   Class _____   Date _____

Historical Background for
A Home in the Wilderness Part 1:
Preparations

History of the Dutch Colony of New Netherlands

The Florentine explorer Giovanni da Verrazzano was the first documented European explorer to land on Manhattan in April of 1524. He made it to the mouth of the Hudson River before turning back.

Manhattan wasn't mapped out until 1609 when Henry Hudson, an English explorer sailing for the Netherlands, arrived and established contact with the Algonquian-speaking Lenape people living there.

Hudson's goal was to find a Northwest passage through North America to Asia. Manhattan Island, recorded as *Manna-hata*, in officer Robert Juet's logbook.[1]

The island's name originates from the Lenape language Munsee, *manaháhtaan* (where *manah-* means "gather", *-aht-* means "bow", and *-aan* is an abstract element used to form verb stems). A reasonable translation of the Lenape word then is "the place for gathering (wood to make) bows." According to research by Albert Seqaqkind Anthony who recorded Munsee traditions, the island was named for the grove of hickory trees that grew on the southern end of the island. The wood from these trees was used to make bows.[2]

The Dutch established a fur trading settlement on Governor's Island in 1624. Two years later, the Dutch purchased the island of Manhattan and began construction of the harbor town of New Amsterdam.

Coalition War, c. 1625-35. Public Domain.

Purchase of Manhattan

Popular belief says that the frugal Dutch purchased the island for $24 worth of trinkets and glass beads.[3] However, this legend ignores several important factors.

Firstly, it is important to note that the Dutch were foremost traders. They desired peaceable access to trade networks. To that end, they sought a legal transfer of land, rather than a military conquest.

Surviving documents from the West India Company indicate that the company authorized the provisional director, Willem Verhulst, to purchase Manhattan.[4] On November 5, 1626, The Hague reported receiving a communication from the colony stating (in translation) that "They have purchased the Island from the *wilden* for the value of 60 guilders."[5]

[1] Juet, Robert (2006) [1625]. "Juet's Journal of Hudson's 1609 Voyage, from the 1625 Edition of *Purchas His Pilgrimes*". *The New York Times*. Translated by Brea Barthel. p. 16. Archived from the original on July 3, 2016. Retrieved May 11, 2020.

[2] *Goddard, Ives (2010). "The Origin and Meaning of the Name "Manhattan"". New York History.* **91** *(4): 277–293. hdl:10088/16790. ISSN 0146-437X – via Smithsonian Research Online.*

[3] Hsitory.com Editors. *"New Amsterdam becomes New York," History*, A&E Television Networks. May 19, 2023. Retrieved March 15, 2024.

[4] Howe, Richard. "Notes On The Manhattan Purchase," The Gotham Center for New York City History. June 27, 2012. Accessed March 14, 2024.

[5] Janos.NYC, *"Today in NYC History: How the Dutch Actually Bought Manhattan (The Long Version)," Today in NYC History.* N.d. Accessed March 14, 2024.

It was a historian in 1846 who first translated the 60 guilders into $24, but other scholars have since equated the value in today's currency to varying amounts ranging from $1,000, $2,000, or as much as $15,000.[6]

While this might still seem like a steal by today's standards, it should be noted that the Native Americans received tools, iron pots, and other manufactured goods that they were not able to produce themselves, which would have increased their trade value in economic terms.

A second consideration regards whether the Native American representatives had the legal right to transfer the land. This point is harder to prove.

Some historians believe that the Canarsees tribe which was based out of Brooklyn and controlled only the southern tip of Manhattan negotiated the deal without the participation of the Weckquasgeeks, who controlled the rest of the island.[7]

As evidence, they point to the hostilities that developed between the settlers and the northern tribe in the 1640s, known as "Kieft's War."[8]

The last factor to consider is whether the Native Americans understood the type of agreement they were making. Did their concept of land ownership prevent them from understanding the deal the Dutch wanted to make?

It has been commonly taught that Native American tribes did not believe that the land could be owned in the European sense of private ownership, however, new research is questioning this assertion.

Native American tribes claimed communal lands and fought other tribes to defend those ownership rights. This is in part what lead to the confederations, or alliances, between certain tribes against other such confederations.

Additionally, law professor, Robert J. Miller, argues that Native Americans recognized both permanent and semi-permanent ownership of land. The fact that the land was communally owned by the tribe did not prevent family units and clans from acquiring and using exclusive rights to portions of communal land.[9]

The fact that the West India Company continued to peaceably negotiate with the Lenape and succeeded in acquiring full and legal title to parts of Brooklyn, Queens, and Staten Island over the next several decades, supports the notion that the Lenape tribes understood the terms of the deal and chose to sell the land.[10]

Even if they had not understood the terms of the first purchase, they surely would have by the second, third, and fourth transactions.

History of the Lenape Tribe

The Lenni-Lenape Nation, or Delaware people as they are now known, are commonly considered to be the ancestors of the many tribes inhabiting the region encompassing the states of New Jersey and Delaware, the southwestern portion of Pennsylvania lying between the Susquehanna and Delaware rivers, and the southeastern part of New York west of the Hudson River.[11]

Archeologists believe the Lenape people inhabited this region for more than five thousand years, long before the arrival of the Europeans, the birth and death of Christ, or even Abraham, the father of the Hebrew and Arab people.[12]

Many seventeenth century tribes originated from the Lenape, including the Weckquaesgeek (pronounced phonetically), which lived in the northern part of Manhattan. They were also called Manhattans and Wappingers (by the Dutch).

The Weckquaesgeek spoke the Munsee dialect of the Algonquian language and were part of an alliance with the Mohawk in the north.[13]

[6] Howe, ibid; Janos.NYC, ibid; Benchley, Nathaniel. *"The $24 Swindle," American Heritage Magazine,* December 1959. Accessed March 14, 2024.

[7] Benchley, ibid.
[8] Janos.NYC, ibid.
[9] Miller, Robert J. "Economic Development in Indian Country: Will Capitalism or Socialism Succeed?" Oregon Law Review, Vol. 80, No. 3, Fall 2001, pg. 768.

[10] Janos.NYC, ibid.
[11] Alligood, Nekole. "The History of the Delaware Nation," *Delaware Nation.* Web. Accessed 4/9/2024.
[12] Cohen, Doris Darlington. "The Weckquaesgeek," with verbal guidance from Nicholas Shoumatoff, Curator and Delaware Expert at Ward Pound Trailside Museum and his library, pg. 1
[13] Alligood, ibid.

The lower Hudson River area where they lived was very hospitable environment. It was rich in fish, shellfish, game, edible and medicinal plants. The waterways facilitated transportation and trade networks. The land was fertile for planning crops and finding flint, used for arrowheads.[14]

They were a peaceful people and largely stayed in one place, migrating only seasonally from the southeastern part of New York to Manhattan to fish and gather the shells used to make wampum. They had largely varied diet consisting of fish, shellfish, game, such as, deer, elk, bear, turkey, snakes, frogs, and beaver, as well as cultivated crops, like corn, squash, and beans, and gathered berries, nuts, and root vegetables. Men did the hunting and fishing, while the women gathered, planted, and harvested the crops.[15]

Women were responsible for making all the clothing, adornments, and household goods. They tanned animal pelts for clothing, moccasins, blankets, and coverings for their winter houses, known as *Nash Wetu*. They made clay pottery and used turkey feathers woven together to make lighter weight blankets. They wove reeds into mats to line the inside walls and floors or for making baskets for carrying and storing goods.[16]

The men cleared the forest using a slash and burn method of stripping the bark around the base of trees and setting fires around the tree to fell it. Large trees were made into dugout canoes for fishing in Long Island Sound and the Atlantic Ocean. The bark was used for lighter-weight canoes, used for long-distance travel in the calmer rivers. They used bent saplings to make domed bark-covered houses and sleeping platforms along the inside walls of the homes. They also made lean-tos for summer shade that captured the cooling breezes.[17]

The Town of Pomieock, by Spenser Nicols.
Library of Congress

Men also made weapons and tools from wood, bone, shell, and flint rock. They also carved the wampum beads from the oyster shells for use in making jewelry, belts, and trade.[18]

The men shaved the sides of their heads with a coxcomb (like the comb of a male rooster), or mohawk, in the front and long hair in the back. They often added feathers or a fox tail hanging down the back.

The men plucked their beards and painted their faces in colors of blue, black, yellow, white, or red for ceremonies and warfare. They wore beaded necklaces of copper, wampum, shell, and stone.[19]

Women had long black hair worn straight or in braids, often tied with strings or shells. Sometimes they cut bangs across their foreheads. They wore headbands or small square caps. They wore beaded girdles around their slim waists.[20]

---

[14] Cohen, ibid.
[15] Cohen, ibin.
[16] Cohen, ibin, pgs 5-6.
[17] Cohen, ibin.

[18] Cohen, ibin., pg. 2
[19] Cohen, ibin, pg. 4
[20] Cohan, ibin.

Name _____ Date _____

Discussion Questions

Student Instructions: On the back of this page or a separate sheet of answer the following questions. Be prepared to discuss them with the class. Make sure to put your full name and the date at the top of your answer page.

Vocabulary Assignment: Underline all the words that appear to be technical history terms. (*Scaffolded: Use the highlighted words*.) Whether or not you are already familiar with the word, notice the context around the word to create a guess definition for the word. After that, look up the word in the dictionary and write the exact, relevant definition(s) below your guess.

1. What is the primary purpose of this text (informative, persuasive/argumentative, entertaining)? Does the author(s) reveal his/her bias (opinion) about the Dutch or the Native Americans? If so, what is their bias, and how do you know? If not, how did they maintain a neutral tone? Use textual evidence to support your point.

4. Based on the information in the text, what were the two reasons the Dutch came to the region of North America that became New Netherlands?

5. In your own words, describe the three factors that must be considered in judging the fairness of the Dutch purchase of Manhattan.

6. Based on the evidence provided, do you think the Dutch believed that they had made a fair trade in buying Manhattan? Why or why not?

7. Based on the evidence provided, do you think the Native Americans believed they had made a fair trade in selling Manhattan? Why or why not? Be sure to consider how confusions between the different tribes inhabiting the land may had affected the deal.

8. According to the text, the Weckquaesgeek people living on Manhattan formed alliances with the Mohawk tribes further north. Provide at least two reasons to explain why groups of people or nations form alliances. What does this tell us about the relationships between the various Native American tribes living on the Eastern coast of North America? Explain your answer.

9. What roles and responsibilities did Native American men have within their families and tribe? What roles and responsibilities did women have?

10. Explain why Native American societies would be organized based on gender roles in this way. Support your answer with evidence.

24

Teacher's Section!!

Completeness _____

Comprehension_____

Clarity/Legibility_____

Total Score: _____

Name _____

Class _____

Date _____

Discussion Questions Prologue and Chapter 1

Student Instructions: On the back of this page or a separate sheet of answer the following questions. Be prepared to discuss them with the class. Make sure to put your full name and the date at the top of your answer page.

1. Fire is used symbolically throughout this novel. What meaning(s) might the fire represent in the prologue?

11. What significance do wampum belts have in Alsoomse's society? Why might tribal leaders use them to "tell stories"? What does this tell us about their societies?

12. The first paragraph, which takes place later in the story, serves as foreshadowing for the rest of the book. What is foreshadowing? How does the author use this technique to draw readers into the story?

13. Describe the narrator in your own words. What details does the author provide in the text and what do they tell the reader about his personality, and other physical, mental, or emotional characteristics?

14. How does the setting (time and place) of this story relate to the historical summary? Where and when in the series of events listed in the historical summary does this story fit in? What facts do you learn about the Dutch colony and their relationship with the Native tribes in the immediate area. Use textual evidence from both the story and historical summary to support your answer.

Name _____

Class _____

Date _____

Discussion Questions Chapters 2-3

Student Instructions: On the back of this page or a separate sheet of answer the following questions. Be prepared to discuss them with the class. Make sure to put your full name and the date at the top of your answer page.

1. Based on what you read, did the settlers in New Harlem have a legitimate fear of a possible attack by native tribes? Why or why not?

15. From the clues given in the chapter, what can you infer about the relationships between the Dutch settlers in Wiltwyck and the native tribes in the area? Why do you think the Esopus attacked the settlement of Wiltwyck? What do you think they were hoping to gain?

16. What reasons did Mr. Gayneau give for not wanting to fight? What was he willing to do for his community? Do you think Etienne's father was a coward? Why or why not?

17. Why do you think Etienne made the same decision his father made? Was he just going along with what his father wanted, or did he have his own reason for making that decision? Explain.

18. Why didn't the settlers go to war immediately? What two things did they do first? What does that imply about their life on Manhattan prior to the attack on Wiltwyck?

26

Name _____

Class _____

Date _____

Discussion Questions Chapter 4

Student Instructions: On the back of this page or a separate sheet of answer the following questions. Be prepared to discuss them with the class. Make sure to put your full name and the date at the top of your answer page.

1. What skills did Etienne learn from his Lenape friends? Why were those important lessons? How would they help him in the new world?

2. What natural resources did the Lenape use in making tools, weapons, and means of transportation?

3. The colonists had their own rowboats. Why would they value the native-made canoes so highly? Have you ever been in a rowboat or a canoe or kayak? If so, consider the differences between these types of boats in terms of maneuverability, stability, and ease of use.

Discussion Questions Chapter 5

Student Instructions: On the back of this page or a separate sheet of answer the following questions. Be prepared to discuss them with the class. Make sure to put your full name and the date at the top of your answer page.

1. In the beginning of chapter 5, Etienne repeats a Lenape story about how wolves and dogs became enemies. Later, Noshi tells two more mythic stories. Has anyone ever told you stories, myths, or fairytales? What kinds of lessons did you learn from them? Thinking about the myths in this chapter and the ones you have been told, what roles do stories such as these serve in communities? Explain your answer.

19. In Lenape culture, animals represented different traits and skills. What was a spirit animal? Why would it have been important for boys becoming men to find their spirit animal? What other important skills did boys have to demonstrate in their coming-of-age ceremonies?

20. The wolf and the eagle are used symbolically throughout this book. What might Etienne's confrontation with the wolf mean? Explain your answer with evidence from the chapter.

21. The colonists used local trees to build their stockades, just as the Lenape did. Compare the methods the colonists used with those of the natives in felling and shaping trees. Which method was more effective? Which method was easier? Explain your answers.

22. What purpose did tobacco pipes and smoke houses play in Lenape society? How did the methods of negotiating peace differ between the Dutch and Lenape people? How could these differences lead to misunderstandings or miscommunications? Explain your answer.

28

Name _____

Class _____

Date _____

Discussion Questions Chapter 6

Student Instructions: On the back of this page or a separate sheet of answer the following questions. Be prepared to discuss them with the class. Make sure to put your full name and the date at the top of your answer page.

1. The first two sentences which describe Etienne's dream, is used as foreshadowing. What is foreshadowing? How does this technique add to the suspense of the story?

2. How does the author make use of symbolism in this passage? Why is Etienne depicted as a wolf? What is the author trying to say about Etienne by using this depiction? Do you think the fire is a literal fire or is it symbolic? If it is symbolic, what does it represent? Can the fire be both symbolic and literal? Why or why not?

3. Etienne's father is a pacifist. Look up the definition for this word and write it down. Does this make him a coward? Etienne is struggling with his father's stance on war. Is there ever a time to fight, or should war be avoided at all costs? Explain your answer.

4. Alsoomse is struggling to accept her gender-based role in the tribe. Early societies across Eurasia, Africa, Oceania, and the Americas all break down familial and societal duties based largely on gender, though there are a few exceptions. Why are gender-based roles so common in societies?

5. Kitchi asks Etienne why his people came to North America and why they ask the native tribes to change, when many of them fled their homes because they did not want to change their religion. Why do you think people so often mistreat others the very same way they have been mistreated?

Name _____

Class _____

Date _____

Discussion Questions Chapter 7

Student Instructions: On the back of this page or a separate sheet of answer the following questions. Be prepared to discuss them with the class. Make sure to put your full name and the date at the top of your answer page.

1. Alsoomse often acts impulsively. List at least three times when she acts without thinking. Are there consequences when she acts this way? Why or why not? If there are consequences, would you classify them as generally good or bad? Explain.

2. Evaluate Hassun's objections to Kitchi's plan of scaling the palisades? Are they valid, in other words, do they have merit? Why do you think Hassun is willing to follow his younger brother's suggestions? What abilities does Kitchi bring to this rescue operation? What skills and experiences does Hassun have? What strengths does Alsoomse have?

3. The willow tree is often given human characteristics in this story. This is called anthropomorphism. Etienne also interacted with a willow tree in chapter 3. Based on these two scenes, what purpose does the willow tree serve in this story? What does it represent or symbolize?

30

Name _____

Class _____

Date _____

Discussion Questions Chapter 8

Student Instructions: On the back of this page or a separate sheet of answer the following questions. Be prepared to discuss them with the class. Make sure to put your full name and the date at the top of your answer page.

1. Does Etienne learn any useful information in this chapter? Explain.

2. One of the soldiers mentions that the War Council had approved the commander's ruling prohibiting soldiers from drinking alcohol. Why do you think the commander would make this ordinance? Support your answer with evidence from the chapter.

3. What rules are you required to follow, either at home, school, clubs, sports, or other organizations. Why do you think those rules are there? What purpose do they serve?

Name _____

Class _____

Date _____

Trading Simulation

Teacher Instructions: Divide the class into two groups. Give each group one of the Background sheets following and a copy of the discussion questions. Tell students to take a few moments to examine their information and answer the questions below (provide copies of the questions to each group.

Note: If you have a large class, you can create two or three groups for each background type, for more student engagement, and then pair one of each type of group together for the second part of the simulation.

1. Choose a name for your group.

2. What resources are you good at producing? What are you inefficient at producing?

3. What resources do you need to survive the winter? What resources do you have?

4. Can you survive the winter with what you have?

5. If you could improve your situation, what would you improve?

6. What could you trade to improve your lifestyle?

Now have the two groups talk to each other and compare their resources and abilities. Ask the groups to answer the following questions.

7. What does the other group do better than your own group?

8. If they could make a trade with the other group, would they be able to improve their lifestyle?

Tell the groups that they are going to make a trade with the other group, but that they can only make the trade if it improves their situation. They must still be able to provide for their essential needs.

Give the groups time to make the trade.

After the trade is made, recall the class, and ask:

9. How did trading with the other group benefit your group?

10. What must be true for two groups to want to make a trade?

Group 1 Background

Student Instructions: Read the information below. When you are finished answer the questions that follow.

Your group has lived on this land for many generations. Your women have learned how to grow corn, beans, and squash that are well adapted to this environment and with very little effort.

In the Spring, after the snow melts, you plant the crops in the cleared fields and let the rains water them. Your children sit on platforms around the fields to scare away the birds and rabbits. Once the seeds have sprouted and are growing strongly, you can leave the crops to grow on their own. You will return in the Fall to harvest the crop.

You count your harvest and discover that, after saving enough seed for the spring planting, you have 1000 pounds of food. You only need 500 pounds of food to feed your group through the next harvest.

While the women are tending the crops, the men make arrows with obsidian tips for hunting, axes with stone heads to be used for making new canoes, clearing fields, and other necessities. Obsidian is rare and difficult to find. It is also controlled by other tribes, who demand tribute for supplying it. Wars have been fought over the control of this resource.

It takes many days to fell a single large tree by removing the bark around its base and using fire to burn the base so that the tree will fall. Then it takes many more weeks of hard work to hollow out the tree to make a canoe.

In the evenings, you spend many hours making arrow heads, shafts, and fleshing for arrows. Then on a hunt, it may take many days and many arrows to bring down a deer or elk. Often when a deer is shot, it then runs, and you must track it down before you can release more arrows to bring it down.

When the animal is finally dead, you must skin it using obsidian knives, clean out the entrails, and cut it into pieces that you can carry.

Group 2 Background

Student Instructions: Read the information below. When you are finished answer the questions that follow.

Your group has recently arrived in this new land. The food you brought with you on the voyage is now gone. You spent the first several weeks chopping down trees to build homes and fences, while clearing fields for planting.

While you brought seeds of wheat, barley, lettuce, cabbage, broccoli, cauliflower, parsnips, beets, carrots, and asparagus with you, your arrival late in the season means that you were unable to grow enough crops to support your community until the next harvest season. You don't want to eat the seeds because you will need them to grow crops next year.

You have been somewhat successful hunting in the woods close to your home, but fear running out of food before winter is over.

You did bring a surplus supply of iron farming tools, knives, cooking pots, guns, and ammunition knowing that it would be months before you could obtain more of these manufactured goods from Europe. And while these tools have been very helpful in quickly felling trees, building homes, and clearing fields, they have not helped the crops grow faster or stronger.

While the men have been felling trees, building structures, clearing fields and hunting, your women have been caring for children and the surviving pigs, cows, and chickens. Additionally, they have been setting up house in temporary shelters or newly constructed wooden homes, making mattresses stuffed with dried grasses or plucked fowl. They also must haul water, mend worn clothing, and find ways to stretch their remaining food stuffs.

Group Discussion Questions:

1. Choose a name for your group.

2. What resources are you good at producing? What are you inefficient at producing?

3. What resources do you need to survive the winter? What resources do you have?

4. Could you survive the winter with what you have? Explain.

5. If you could improve your situation, what would you improve?

6. What could trade to improve your lifestyle?

After meeting with the other group answer the following questions.

7. What does the other group do better than your own group?

8. If your group could make a trade with the other group, would they be able to improve their lifestyle?

Name _____

Class _____

Date _____

Essay Prompt

Continuity and Change Over Time

Student Instructions: Write an essay answering the following prompt. Be prepared to discuss it with the class. Make sure to put your full name and the date at the top of your answer page.

After completing the Trade Simulation, write an essay describing the continuities and change over time for your assigned societies lifestyle resulting from trade. Consider their lifestyle before and after trade networks were established. Also, explain how trade networks were established. Support your answer with specific evidence. Finally, make a conclusion stating your opinion on whether your society was better off before or after trading and why.

36

Teacher's Section!!

Preparation & Collaboration: _____

Content & Completion: _____

Presentation & Articulation: _____

Total Score: _____

Research Project

Student Instructions: As individuals or in groups, follow the instructions below to research one Native American tribe and create your own exhibit to present what you learned.

1. Choose one of the following Native American tribes to research. Use your textbook, the library, or Internet to conduct your research. Be sure to include your sources cited in proper MLA or APA style. Use MyBib (https://www.mybib.com), if you don't know how to do this.

    Note: The Leni-Lenape and Mohawk are from the Northern Woodlands region, which is not included below. For this project, each group should choose a tribe from a different region than the other groups. Note: the following are only a sampling of tribes from each area.

Southeast	**Great Plains**	**Southwest**	**Great Basin**	**NW Coast**
Cherokee	Sioux	Hope	Shoshoni	Chinook
Choctaw	Cheyenne	Navajo	Ute	Tillamook
Chickasaw	Kiowa	Pima	Palute	Quinault
Natchez	Osage	Apache	Bannock	Umpaqua

Plateau	**California**
Nez Perce	Modoc
Flathead	Pomo
Yakima	Costanoan

2. Answer the following for each tribe:

    a. Socioeconomic Characteristics: Where did they live? What was their lifestyle like? What did they eat? How did they get food? What did they wear? What was their house like? Did they play games or have competitions? Did they trade with other groups of people? If so, what did they trade and what did they get in exchange?

    b. Cultural or Religious Characteristics: What or whom did they worship? Was there a religious leader? What did he/she do? What rituals did they have? Did they have any important myths? What were they?

    c. Political Characteristics: How was their tribe's leadership organized? Did they have a single leader or a group leading? What were the leadership roles? Did they have alliances with other tribes? If so, with whom were they aligned and how was the alliance structured? What did each member have to do? What did they get in return?

    d. What did you learn that was interesting or surprising?

3. Locate the region where your tribe lived on a map of the United States. Lightly shade in the region where they lived. What geographical features are in the area? What kind of weather

conditions would they have faced? How did they adapt to these conditions with the resources they had available?

4. Create an exhibit. This can be a diorama, a presentation board, poster, or other creative project to demonstrate what you have learned.

5. Be prepared to present your findings to the class.

6. Take notes as the other students present their research. Note: it might be useful to make a comparison chart to easily see the similarities and differences between each tribe.

7. Questions for Discussion:

   a. What characteristics did Native American tribes from the same region have in common? What characteristics were different? What might explain these similarities and differences?

   b. Did Native American groups from different regions have any characteristics in common? What major differences were there? What might explain these similarities and differences?

   c. Did any of these Native American tribes trade with other groups? With whom did they trade? Do you notice any patterns in their trade networks? Did they trade with people who were close by or far away?

   d. What conclusions can you make about the way native peoples lived in North America?

Essay Prompt

Compare and Contrast

Student Instructions: Write an essay answering the following prompt. Be prepared to discuss it with the class. Make sure to put your full name and the date at the top of your answer page.

After listening to the class presentations, compare and contrast the different tribal communities. How were the societies similar? How were they different? Consider the gender roles, governmental/ leadership structures, economies (what did they produce, what did they trade), religious beliefs, and other cultural considerations. Support your answer with specific evidence from the presentations and exhibits.

Part 2: Rescue

Objectives:

Interpret visual sources to understand historical context.

Interpret primary and secondary sources and analyze the purpose of each type of source.

Compare and contrast primary and secondary sources and analyze the purpose each type of source.

Evaluate the accuracy and usefulness of secondary sources in understanding historical events.

Understand the purpose of narratives in disseminating information.

Handouts:

- *A Home in the Wilderness*, Image 2
- Historical Background for Part 2 with Discussion Questions .
- Discussion Questions by chapter
- Comparing Primary Sources to Historical Retellings
- Analytical Essay

Day 1-2

1. **Bell Ringer:** Students will examine the image in the handout *"A Home in the Wilderness,* Image 2"* and answer the questions. Follow up with a discussion of students' answers.

2. Handout to each student a copy of the **"Historical Background for Part 2"** and tell students that as they read, they should note any unfamiliar or important words.

   a. Underline all the words that appear to be technical history terms (Scaffolded: Use the highlighted words). Use the context around the word to create a guess definition then look up the word in the dictionary.

   b. Answer the questions that follow and discuss with class or teacher. **NOTE:** May need a second day for students to finish answering the questions and hold the class discussion.

Days 3 - 9

1. As students read each section (one or more chapters) ask them to answer the corresponding **"Discussion Questions."** Students could read the chapters at home or in class. The discussion questions may be given out after the students had completed the reading or ahead of time.

2. Conduct a full class discussion or small group round table discussions of the questions.

Day 10

1. Creative Writing Essay Prompt
2. Conduct a class discussion of student responses.

Days 11 - 12

1. Students will read the sections provided from the primary source, "Journal of the Second Esopus War: By Capt. Martin Kregier."

2. Have students (individually or in small groups) answer the questions that follow. They will also need to refer to the novel *A Home in the Wilderness* for some of the questions.

3. Conduct a class discussion of students answer to the questions.

Day 13

1. Analytical essay prompt.

Name _____ Class _____ Date _____

A Home in the Wilderness, Image 2

Painting of Fort Wiltwyck, 1695 Kingston, *by Len Tantillo, 2015*
Used with permission.

Answer the following questions:

1. Describe the defensive structures visible in this image.

2. What else do you notice in this image? For example, what can you tell about the layout of the town? What purpose do the structures and fenced areas seem to serve? What types of structures are outside of the town walls? How is the land being used?

3. What can you infer about what life was like living in and around Fort Wiltwyck? Why might some people choose to live outside the fort walls? What might this tell you about their expectations or relationships with surrounding native tribes?

Name _____

Class _____

Date _____

Historical Background for

A Home in the Wilderness Part 2
The Esopus Wars

Earlier Colonial-Native American Wars

From Trade to War

When Europeans began to settle in North America, many native peoples quickly realized the benefits of trade with these newcomers. Still living with Neolithic (new stone age) technology, the native people became dependent upon European manufactured products including iron tools and pots, wool textiles, guns, and alcohol, which they quickly began to abuse.

As more and more Europeans began to arrive in North America and demand more and more land, many native tribes began to push back. The two most well-know of these conflicts are the Jamestown Massacre of 1622 and the Pequot War that took place in New England in the 1630s.

Jamestown Tragedy of 1622

The so-called massacre, uprising, attack or military offense by the Powhatan chiefdom resulted from a buildup of grievances over a thirteen-year period.

Both sides wanted continued beneficial trade relationships. The dispute arose over the colonial desire for increased land expansion to accommodate the additional colonists arriving. This reduced the amount of agricultural land available to the native tribes.

Additionally, the British colonists were more interested in growing tobacco as a cash crop then in growing their own food. So, when a drought hit the region in 1609, the Powhatan Confederacy had little food to trade, so the English began to steal it from the ripening fields.

A second problem was the high rate of disease at Jamestown, which lead John Smith to move colonists to healthier settlements down river and to the west in the heart of Powhatan territory.

The Powhatan responded by surrounding Fort James preventing the colonists from hunting, gathering food, or collecting firewood.

they further demanded that the colonists return to England or at least to confine themselves to Jamestown.

Despite this, tensions continued to build until March 22, 1622, when Powhatan's successor, Chief Opechancanough led his warriors in a military attack on the colonists living along the James River. Groups of warriors appeared at numbers of settlers' homes and fields with the pretense of sharing a meal or trading. Then they unleashed a surprise attack.

It appears that Jamestown was warned by a converted native who alerted the man he worked for, Richard Pace, who then informed the settlement.[21]

Nearly 350 colonial men, women, and children were killed, accounting for a third of the English population. Around 20 women were kidnapped, and many plantations were destroyed and burned.[22]

This attack became a turning point in the relations between the colonists and the native tribes, at the English now determined to lead an outright

---

[21] Nancy D. Egloff, "The Tragedy of 1622: The Powhatan Paramount Chiefdom Military Offensive Against English Settlers in Virginia," Jamestown-Yorktown Foundation, n.d.

[22] W.E. White, "The Anglo-Powhatan War of 1622," Christopher Newport University, n.d.

war against the Powhatan that finally ended in a peace treaty in 1632.

Ultimately, the Powhatan would become a tributary state subordinate to the more powerful English government, who would appoint their high chief, and require the tribe to pay an annual fee of 20 beaver pelts and to provide military assistance against foreign tribes.

Pequot War of the 1630s

As with the Jamestown tragedy, the conflict with the Pequot living in present-day Connecticut was also the result of years of buildup tensions over land, trade, and livestock.[23]

During the 1620s the Dutch and Pequot controlled the trade in the area that would become New England. This control of the trade led the Pequot to attempt to subjugate other tribes throughout the region that would become Connecticut and Rhode Island.

"By 1635, the Pequot extended their political and economic ties through a tributary confederacy using coercion, warfare, diplomacy, and intermarriage."[24]

The arrival of English traders and settlers to the Connecticut valley in the 1630s upset the balance of power, and the subjugated tribes began to trade and ally themselves with the English. The new English-tribal alliances tried to break the Dutch-Pequot control of the trade resulting in pushback.

Tension continued to rise until the summer of 1634 when an English trader and privateer, John Stone, and his crew were killed by the Pequot, who viewed it as a justified action. Then in July of 1636, English trader John Oldham, was killed by the Manisses of Block Island.[25]

This time the English of Massachusetts Bay Colony decided they could not tolerate any more English deaths by the native tribes.

Captain John Endicott and 90 men attacked two seemingly abandoned villages on Block Island and then confronted a Pequot village and attacked it, though most of its inhabitants escaped into the woods. The Pequot retaliated by raiding colonial settlements in the English Connecticut Colony.

As tensions continued to rise, the Narraganset and Mohegan allied with the English against the Pequot.

In May the leaders of many Connecticut towns met in Hartford to raise a militia and placed Captain John Mason in command. Mason set out with 90 militia and 70 Mohegan to attack the Pequot at their fort. He was then joined by John Underhill with another 20 Englishmen.

In an attempt to trick the Pequot spies into thinking they were not planning to attack, Mason and Underhill sailed from Fort Saybrook to Narragansett Bay where they gained the support of 200 Narragansett.

Mason and Underhill then marched their forces to Mistick Fort (present-day Mystic) where they initiated a surprise attack on the Pequot on the pre-dawn morning of May 26, 1637.

The combined English-tribal army surrounded one of the two Pequot fortified villages at Mistick. Only 20 soldiers were able to breach the palisade gate of the Pequot village and were quickly overwhelmed. So, the commanders ordered the use of fire to facilitate their soldiers escape.

T he Pequot village was built of dried bark houses and completely surrounded by a wooden palisade, the fire spread quickly trapping the majority of the Pequot villagers. Those who did manage to escape were killed by the surrounding soldiers and warriors.

Of the estimated 500 Pequot men, women, and children in the village, only seven were captured and seven more escaped into the woods.

The Narragansett and Mohegan allies and many colonists were horrified by the destruction and death of the Pequot women and children.

The combined army pursued the remaining Pequot warriors and refugees, catching up with them in a swamp at Sasqua. The English

[23] "Pequot War – Connecticut History: A CT Humanities Project," n.d.

[24] Mashantucket Pequot Museum & Research Center "Causes of the Pequot War,", n.d. Accessed July 22, 2024.
[25] Ibid.

surrounded the swamp, this time allowing several hundred to surrender, mostly women and children.

The Pequot chief, Sassacus, and around 80 warriors escaped and fled westward and to seek refuge with the Mohawk tribe. Instead, the Mohawk murdered Sassacus and his bodyguard and sent his head and hands to Hartford.[26] This essentially ended the Pequot War.

The Esopus Wars

The Dutch started building a settlements in what is now New York in 1652. They traded with the Native American tribes in the area using the North River, or what we now call the Hudson River.

In 1658, the Dutch moved farther north into the area now known as Kingston and built a fort there. They named their settlement Esopus, after the Munsee-Esopus tribe in the area. Later, in 1661, they later renamed it Wiltyck.[27]

Causes of the Conflict

Though both the Dutch and the Esopus were wary of each other, they commenced trading. The Dutch were particularly interested in the beaver pelts, though they also traded for other animal skins, such as bear and fox.

The Esopus quickly became dependent upon European manufactured goods, including iron axe heads, knives, hoes and cooking pots, copper, wool clothing and blankets, glass beads, and many other items they could not produce themselves.

As the settlement continued to grow and the native tribal numbers were impacted by formerly unknown European diseases, tensions began to increase.

The Esopus hunting grounds were being tapped, so the Esopus began hunting the Dutch pigs, which had been released into the woods to forage. The Dutch demanded payment for the killed pigs, but the Esopus viewed them as fair

hunting game, since they were running free in the forest.

Additionally, the natives began to acquire alcohol and to abuse it. It became so problematic that the leadership of the Dutch colony of New Netherlands outlawed the sale of spirits to the natives. In spite of the order, opportunists continue to sell alcohol to the natives.

The First Esopus War

One night in 1660, after too much drinking, a group of Esopus men became rowdy while celebrating around their campfire.

A group of Dutchmen fearful that the noise signified aggression, attacked a native village. Then 500 Esopus retaliated by laying siege to the fort, destroyed the Dutch crops and killing their cattle.[28]

The Dutch were able to get reinforcements in men and weapons from New Amsterdam and to sign a truce in July of 1660.

Three years of peace followed, although disagreements continued over farmland, as the Dutch continued to expand and build the settlement of Niew Dorp, or "New Village" (now Hurley).[29]

The Second Esopus War

On the morning of June 7, 1663, the Esopus decided to try to push the Dutch out of the region, by planning an ambush. They approached the open gates of Niew Dorp and Wiltyck under the pretense of wanting to trade.

Niew Dorp was the first to be attacked. Once inside the settlement, the Esopus attacked, burning houses, killing, and kidnapping women and children. Some riders were sent to Wiltwyck for help.

Captain Martin Kregier reports in his *Journal of the Second Esopus War*, that groups of Esopus entered through all the gates, "divided themselves among all the houses and dwellings in

[26] "Of Plymouth Plantation: Early American Digital Archive (EADA)." Archived from the original on 2018-06-25. Retrieved July 22, 2024.
[27] David Levine, *Hudson Valley*, "The Esopus Wars: A History of the Battle Between the Dutch and Local

American Indians in the 1660s," 10/23/2013. Accessed 5/10/2020.
[28] David Levine, ibid.
[29] Marc B. Fried, *The Early History of Kingston & Ulster County, NY.* Marbletown, Kingston, NY: Ulster County Historical Society, 1975.

44

a friendly manner, having with them a little maize some few beans to sell to our Inhabitants, by which means they kept them within their houses, and thus went from place to place as spies to discover our strength in man."[30]

About a half an hour later the men from Niew Dorp arrived through the windmill gate exclaiming "The Indians have destroyed the New Village?"[31]

In Wiltwyck, twelve men, four women, and two children were killed. Another ten women and children were kidnapped, and twelve homes were burned. In Niew Dorp, three men were killed, and eight women and 26 children were taken prisoner, while the entire village was burned to the ground.

This was the start of the Second Esopus War, which rocked the entire colony of New Netherlands. In response stockades were built around the village of New Harlem on the northern tip of Manhattan. Soldiers and weapons were sent north from New Amsterdam. The militia was called up in New Harlem, trained, and sent to support Wiltwyck. New Harlem was also sent cannon to defend themselves, as well as weapons for the militia.[32]

Native tribes also began taking sides. The Weckquaesgeeks (also called the Wappingers by the Dutch) were a Munsee-speaking tribe related to the Lenape, as were the Esopus. In spite of this they choose to side with the Dutch along with the Mohawk, in order to protect their trade.

The Esopus and their hostages retreated into the forest and enlisted the support of the Minisink tribe. They carried out guerilla-style warfare against the Dutch and kept moving their camps to stay out of sight of the Dutch.[33]

The Dutch led several assaults against the Esopus but were seldom able to find them. In frustration, they started burning abandoned Esopus forts and corn fields. In September of 1663, the Dutch finally found the new Esopus camp and killed many natives, including their chief Papequanaehen, which effectively ended the war, although there were still a few skirmishes and hostages to be returned. [34]

A few Mohawk and Wappinger men were sent to find the Esopus and to negotiate for the return of the Dutch women and children. These negotiations did lead to the eventual return of all the hostages on both sides.[35]

Many of the Dutch hostages reported that they'd been treated well. A few even grew fond of their captors. According to Marc Fried, "There were two children who had become caregivers for an elderly woman, and they stayed with her for some time."[36]

A peace treaty was signed by all parties in Fort Wiltwyck in 1664.

This conflict can be seen as a turning point in colonial history. It changed the largely peaceful trade-based coexistence between the Dutch colonists and the surrounding native tribes. Some historians cite this event as one of the reasons the Dutch gave up their colony so easily to the British in 1664, allowing Great Britian control of trade with the remaining tribes for the Eastern woodlands and the major ports in North America.

This shift in economic power would see the decline of the Dutch as a global economic powerhouse and allow the British to fund their wars with France to become the dominate world power for the next two centuries.

[30] Capt. Martin Kregier, *Journal of the Second Esopus War: With an account of the Massacre at Wiltwyck, the names of those killed, wounded, and taken prisoners, by the Indians of that occasion, 1663.* Translated from the original Dutch MS.
[31] Ibid.

[32] Jaap Jacobs, *The Colony of New Netherland: A Dutch Settlement in Sevententh-Century America.* Ithaca, NY: Cornwell University, 2009.
[33] David Levine.
[34] Capt. Martin Kregier.
[35] Ibid.
[36] Marc B. Fried.

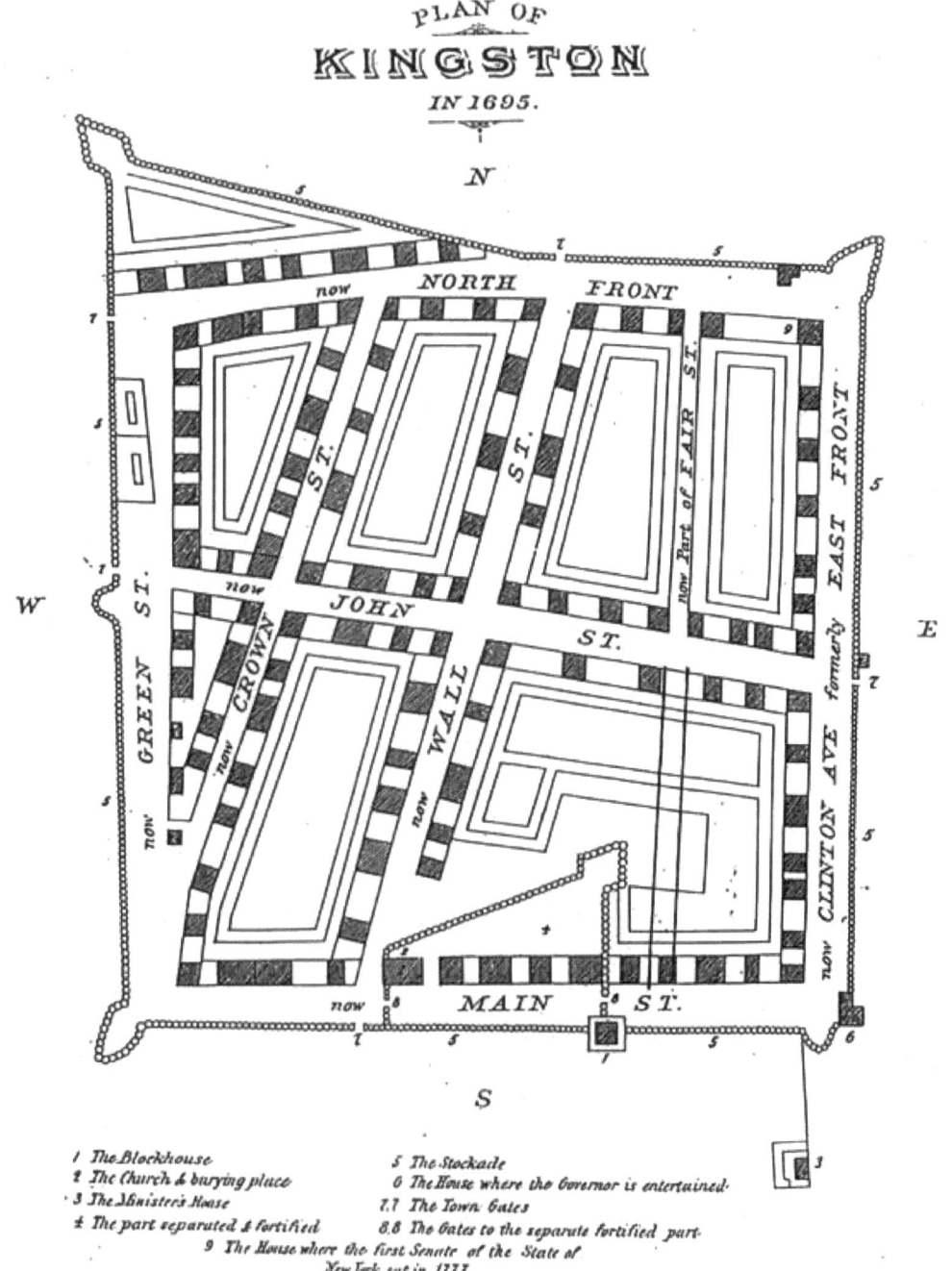

PLAN OF
KINGSTON
IN 1695.

N

1 The Blockhouse
2 The Church & burying place
3 The Ministre's House
4 The part separated & fortified
5 The Stockade
6 The House where the Governor is entertained
7.7 The Town Gates
8.8 The Gates to the separate fortified part
9 The House where the first Senate of the State of New York sat in 1777.

MILLER MAP OF KINGSTON STOCKADE AREA IN 1695
AS DESIGNATED BY GOVERNOR PETRUS STUYVESANT
***
Documents Relative to the Colonial History of New York State,
Insert between pages 84,85, Vol. XIII

Brodhead, John Romeyn, et. Al. "Miller Map of Kingston Stockade Area in 1695 as Designated by Governor Petrus Stuyvesant." *Documents Relative to the Colonial History of the State of New-York: Procured in Holland, England, and France*, Vol. XIII, Albany: Weed, Parsons, 1853.
Ulster County Archives

Name _____ Class _____ Date _____

Discussion Questions
Compare and Contrast: Early Colonial – Native American Wars

Student Instructions: On the back of this page or on a separate piece of paper, answer the following questions. Support your answers with evidence from the reading above. Be prepared to discuss your answers with the class.

Vocabulary Assignment: Underline all the words that appear to be technical history terms (Scaffolded: Use the highlighted words). Whether or not you are already familiar with the word, read the context around the word to create develop a guess definition for the word. After that, look up the word in the dictionary and write the exact, relevant definition(s) below your guess.

1. Create a Venn diagram or other visual aid to compare the similarities and differences in the causes of the Jamestown Tragedy, the Pequot War, and the Esopus Wars. List all the specific causes for each conflict in the appropriate place on your diagram.

2. Write a paragraph summarizing your evidence from above. Where the causes for each conflict similar in each case, or not? Were there any significant differences? If so, what were they and what might explain these differences?

3. Compare the dates for each conflict to the dates each colony was founded. How long did it take from the founding of each colony until the conflict broke out in each? How do these numbers compare? Do you see any trends or similarities? What might explain these findings?

4. What strategies did the different Native American tribes use in each conflict? What strategies did the colonial armies use in each conflict? Consider the use of allies, types of weapons, military tactics, and other factors.

5. What resulted from each conflict? Which side won? What happened to the losing side? What factors explain these results?

6. How did these conflicts impact the areas where they were fought? In other words, considering what life was like in these regions before the conflicts and what it was like after the conflicts, why are these conflicts considered to be "turning points in history"? Explain your answer.

Name _____

Class _____

Date _____

Discussion Questions Chapter 9

Student Instructions: On the back of this page or a separate sheet of answer the following questions. Be prepared to discuss them with the class. Make sure to put your full name and the date at the top of your answer page.

1. This is the second chapter to be told from Alsoomse's perspective. Review chapter 7 again. What method does the author use to distinguish Alsoomse's chapters from those told by Etienne? (Hint: Which narrative style is used: first person, third person close, or third person omniscient?) Use evidence to support your answer.

2. How does the author's use of different narrative styles change the relationship the reader has with the characters, or does it? Explain your answer.

3. Why do you think the author uses this technique when shifting character perspectives? Do you think it is effective? Why or why not?

4. Think about the character of Hassun. How does he feel about Etienne? What actions or events might have caused him to feel this way? Is he justified in feeling this way? Why or why not? Do you think he is treating Etienne fairly? Why or why not?

48

Name _____

Class _____

Date _____

Discussion Questions Chapters 10 & 11

Student Instructions: On the back of this page or a separate sheet of answer the following questions. Be prepared to discuss them with the class. Make sure to put your full name and the date at the top of your answer page.

1. Why did the Dutch let Noshi, the Mohawks and Etienne go? What were they supposed to do?

2. What information does the reader learn from Kanti about the different tribes in the area and their plans? What does the reader learn about the Dutch their knowledge of the area and surrounding tribes, and their actions in this conflict?

3. What do you think explains the actions of the Dutch when they come to Kanti's village?

4. Why might the Dutch have a difficult time determining which tribes or villages were hostile, friendly, or neutral?

5. Put yourselves in the shoes of the Dutch settlers. How would they have felt when the Esopus attacked their settlements? Would they have felt the attack was warranted, or justified? Why or why not? If your sister or mother was taken hostage, what would you be willing to do to get her back?

6. Now put yourself in the moccasins of the Esopus. Did they feel justified in attacking the Dutch settlements? Why or why not? Suppose you went to visit your grandmother for the summer and then came home to find someone else living in your house. You can't get them out because the law says they have a right to stay. How would you feel? What would you be willing to do to get them to leave?

7. How do the different perspectives of this conflict, as seen in the war council meeting and Kanti's retelling compare? How does it broaden your understanding of this conflict?

Teacher's Section!!

Completeness _____

Comprehension_____

Clarity/Legibility_____

Total Score: _____

Name _____

Class _____

Date _____

Discussion Questions Chapter 12

Student Instructions: On the back of this page or a separate sheet of answer the following questions. Be prepared to discuss them with the class. Make sure to put your full name and the date at the top of your answer page.

1. Read Genesis 1 and 2. If you do not have a Bible, you can read a copy at https://www.biblegateway.com. (I recommend using either the English Standard Version or the New International Version, or New Living Translation for easier readability.)

   List the similarities and differences between the creation story in Genesis and the Algonquian version Alsoomse told. Why do you think these stories are so similar? What may explain the differences?

2. Etienne tells the story of the fall of Adam and Eve in the garden. (You can find this story in Genesis 3). How did evil enter the world according to Alsoomse's story? How did evil enter the world according to the Algonquian story? Who is to blame for evil entering the world in each story? How might these differences affect or influence the religious practices or beliefs of each society?

50

Name _____

Class _____

Date _____

Discussion Questions Chapters 13 & 14

Student Instructions: On the back of this page or a separate sheet of answer the following questions. Be prepared to discuss them with the class. Make sure to put your full name and the date at the top of your answer page.

1. What were the different attitudes about the Indians you saw expressed by the colonists in these chapters? What were the different attitudes about the colonists you saw expressed by Native Americans? Why do you think there were so many different opinions? Which were right and which were wrong? Or did each opinion have valid points? Where did they go too far or fail to consider the other groups perspectives?

2. Now think about conflicts with which you are familiar today. The conflicts can be political viewpoints, religious disagreements, arguments between family or friends, sports rivalries, or the like. What valid points does each party or side of the argument/discussion make? Where does each side go too far or fail to consider their opponents perspective?

3. Based on your conclusions, how do you think we can do a better job of solving our conflicts?

Name _____

Class _____

Date _____-_____

Discussion Questions Chapters 15 - 17

Student Instructions: On the back of this page or a separate sheet of answer the following questions. Be prepared to discuss them with the class. Make sure to put your full name and the date at the top of your answer page.

1. Think of a time when you did something rash, or without thinking. How did it turn out? Did your actions have an impact or effect on other people? How did your actions effect you? What did you learn from your experience?

2. In what ways did Etienne react impulsively in these chapters? What impact did his actions have on other people? How did his actions affect himself? What, if anything, should he have done differently? What, if anything, did he do right?

3. Look up the definition for "impulse" and write down what you find. Are impulses good or bad? Explain. Think about what you learned from the experience you described in the first question. How do our past experiences shape our impulses?

52

Name _____

Class _____

Date _____-_____

Discussion Questions Chapters 18 - 19

Student Instructions: On the back of this page or a separate sheet of answer the following questions. Be prepared to discuss them with the class. Make sure to put your full name and the date at the top of your answer page.

1. In chapter 18, Alsoomse is amazed to realize that her little brother Kitchi had grown into a strong and confident warrior. Go back and review the second part of chapter 5 to the end of the chapter. In your own words write a description of Kitchi. What does he look like? What is his personality like? What is his relationship with Etienne, Hassun, Noshi, and Alsoomse like?

2. Now review chapters 18 and 19. How has Kitchi changed? How has his relationship with his father and siblings changed? What clues does the author give to show the reader how Kitchi has grown up?

3. Now examine at the character of Alsoomse. How has she changed from the beginning of the story? How has her relationship with her father and brothers changed? Her father used to tolerate her willfulness. How has he reacted to her recent rebelliousness? What might explain this change?

Name _____

Class _____

Date _____-_____

Discussion Questions Chapters 20 - 21

Student Instructions: On the back of this page or a separate sheet of answer the following questions. Be prepared to discuss them with the class. Make sure to put your full name and the date at the top of your answer page.

1. In chapter 20, Alsoomse tells another story from her people's mythology. What purpose does this story seem to have? Why do you think the author included it in this chapter?

2. Native Americans were known to enter colonists house and spend the night uninvited, especially in homes of colonists friendly to them and living apart from larger settlements or in the wilderness areas. In chapter 21, how does Etienne's mother react to having visitors in her home unexpectedly?

3. Why does Etienne's father decide to leave the sachem and his warriors in his house and goes to bring the leaders of New Harlem back with him, rather than simply taking the Native Americans to the town council?

4. What information was exchanged in the meeting? What concessions did each party ask for? How did the colonists and the Lenape seal the deal they made? What items and/or promises were exchanged?

54

Name _____

Class _____

Date _____

Essay Prompt
Creative Writing

Student Instructions: Write an essay answering the following prompt. Make sure to put your full name and the date at the top of your answer page.

Cultures around the world created myths to explain how the world came into existence, how man was created, or other realities of their world. Create your own myth to explain how something, perhaps an animal, a place, or a community, came to be.

Name _____

Class _____

Date _____

Teacher's Section!!

Introduction: _____

Narrative: _____

Organization: _____

Language: _____

Total Score: _____

Comparing Primary Sources to Historical Retellings

Student Instructions: Read pages 11-12 from the "Journal of the Second Esopus War: By Capt. Martin Kregier" available at https://www.amandamcetas.com/supplemental-materials. Compare the events as they are told in the Journal to the author's retelling in chapters part 2 of *A Home in the Wilderness.* Answer the following questions.

4. Examine the information provided in the Journal about the Council of War on July 16th and compare it to the information given in chapter 10. What details or facts did the author include? What facts or details did she leave out?

5. Now look at the rescue attempt detailed in the Journal on July 20th and compare it to the author's retelling in chapters 11 and 12. What details or facts did the author include in her story? What details did she add to the story?

6. How accurate do you think the author's retelling of these events is? Explain your answer.

7. Which version of the events, the primary source or the retelling, is more interesting to read? Which version made a greater impact on you? Why?

8. What is the purpose of Captain Kregier's Journal of the Second Esopus War? Who is the intended audience? (Who was it written for?)

9. What is the purpose of *A Home in the Wilderness*? Who is her intended audience?

56

Name _____

Class _____

Date _____

Analytical Essay

Student Instructions: Using your answers from "Comparing Primary Sources and Historical Retellings" and information from both documents, answer the question below. Be sure to support your conclusions with specific evidence.

How does purpose and audience affect the writing style, type of information and details included in a historical document compared to a work of historical fiction?

Part 3: Negotiating Peace

Objectives:

Interpret visual sources to understand historical context.

Interpret primary and secondary sources.

Compare and contrast primary and secondary sources and analyze the purpose of each type of source.

Evaluate the accuracy and usefulness of secondary sources in understanding historical events.

Understand the social, economic, political, and cultural practices of the Eastern Woodland Native American groups and the early European colonies.

Understand early colonial relationships with Native American groups.

Understand how and why people have developed methods for measuring time through different historical periods.

Understand the physical properties that allow people to use the sun to measure time.

Handouts:

- *A Home in the Wilderness*, Image 3
- Historical Background Project for Part 3, "Dutch/English and Esopus Peace Agreements" with discussion questions
- *An Agreement made between Richard Nicolls Esq., Governor and the Sachems and the People called the Sopes Indyans. 7th day of October 1665* at the following link: https://clerk.ulstercountyny.gov/sites/default/files/resources/Nicolls%20Esopus%20Peace%20Treaty_2015.pdf
- Discussion Questions by chapter
- Continuity and change over time essay
- Historical Understanding of Time and Development of Clocks with discussion questions
- Sundial Project with questions

Day 1 (May take two days)

1. **Bell Ringer:** Students will examine the image in the handout "*A Home in the Wilderness,* Image 3" and answer the questions. Follow up with a discussion of students' answers.

2. Handout to each student a copy of the **Dutch/English and Esopus Peace Agreements,** a copy of the *An Agreement made between Richard Nicolls Esq., Governor and the Sachems and People called the Sopes Indyans. 7th day of October 1665,* and the discussion questions and tell students that as they read, they should note any unfamiliar or important words.

   a. Underline all the words that appear to be technical history terms (Scaffolded: Use the highlighted words). Use the context around the word to create a guess definition then look up the word in the dictionary.

3. If you have a large class, you may break them into small groups to discuss and answer the questions.

4. Discuss student responses with the class. NOTE: it may take two days to get through this assignment, especially if you have a larger class. In this case plan to discuss student responses on the second day.

Days 2 - 4

1. As students read each section (one or more chapters) ask them to answer the corresponding **"Discussion Questions."** Students could read the chapters at home or in class. The discussion questions may be given out after the students had completed the reading or ahead of time.

2. Conduct a full class discussion or small group round table discussions of the questions.

Day 5

1. Students will answer the continuity and change over time essay prompt.

Day 6 - 7

1. Handout to each student the **Historical Understanding of Time** and **Development of Clocks Timeline** with the discussion questions that follow and give students time to read the material.

2. For larger classes, you may group students into small groups to discuss and answer the questions.

3. After students have completed the questions, discuss their answers (with the class for larger settings). NOTE: with larger classes it is advised to have each group answer a different question.

Sundial Project

1. Gather the required materials and follow the instructions on the handout.

2. A note for teachers follows the instructions to help explain the results of the experiment.

Wrap-up Essay and Book Project Ideas

1. Choose from several essay ideas provided to wrap up the unit.

2. Alternately, choose from the various projects suggested to demonstrate student understanding from the unit.

New Netherlands Map published by Nicolaes Visscher ** (1649-1702).
Media file donated from Koninklijke Bibliotheek, Public Domain

Name _____ Class _____ Date _____

A Home in the Wilderness, Image 3

The Treaty of Pomeiock, by Spencer Nichols. Library of Congress

Answer the following questions:

1. Describe what you see in this image in your own words?

2. Based on this image, what inferences can you make about how the people in this community live, their relationships with other groups of people, their relationships within the community?

3. What specific elements of this image support the conclusions you made in the above question?

Individual/Group Activity (For Teachers)

Research Project Instructions

Teacher Instructions: This is an activity where students will research and share what they have learned about the peace agreement between the Dutch/English colonists and the Esopus tribes. You may download a copy of the original documents with commentary entitled *An Agreement made between Richard Nicolls Esq., Governor and the Sachems and People called the Sopes Indyans. 7th day of October 1665* at the following link: https://clerk.ulstercountyny.gov/sites/default/files/resources/Nicolls%20Esopus%20Peace%20Treaty_2015.pdf.

A copy is also available on the author's website at https://www.amandamcetas.com/supplemental-materials.

1. Have or help students read through the background information on the treaty on pages 7 and 8.

    Ask students to underline or highlight any information that seems important. Tell them to make a note of anything that surprises them, facts that seem to support or conflict with the information provided in the novel, *A Home in the Wilderness*.

2. NOTE: The treaty provided in this document was a renewal of the earlier agreement referenced in the novel as noted on page 8, in the first paragraph midway down it says: "Ruttenber's *Indian Tribes of Hudson's River to 1700,* refers to the Nicolls Treaty *itself* as a renewal of Stuyvesant's 1644 agreement made at Fort Amsterdam."

    Ask students why is it significant, or important, that this treaty was renewed a number of times?

3. Now have students, individually or in small groups, read through the agreement, pages 9-13, and answer the questions provided on the next pages.

Name _____

Class _____

Date _____

Historical Background for
A Home in the Wilderness Part 3:
Dutch/English and Esopus Peace Agreements

1. Read through the background information on the treaty on pages 7 and 8.

   Underline or highlight any information that seems important. Make a note of anything that surprises you, facts that seem to support or conflict with the information provided in the novel, *A Home in the Wilderness.*

2. NOTE: The treaty provided in this document was a renewal of the earlier agreement referenced in the novel as noted on page 8, in the first paragraph midway down it says: "Ruttenber's *Indian Tribes of Hudson's River to 1700,* refers to the Nicolls Treaty *itself* as a renewal of Stuyvesant's 1644 agreement made at Fort Amsterdam."

   Why is it significant, or important, that this treaty was renewed a number of times?

3. Now read through the agreement, pages 9-13, and summarize each provision in your own words.

4. Look through the addendums starting on page 14. How many times was this treaty renewed?

5. What reason is given for the first renewal on April the 11th, 1670?

6. On which renewal date(s) does there appear to be a conflict building, which led the groups to renew the treaty? Support your answer with evidence from the document. In other words, which phrases indicate that there might have been a conflict?

7. Are there any other examples of when additional clarification was given in the renewal document? What needed to be clarified? Why might this have been necessary?

8. On several occasions, a string of wampum was presented during the renewal process. Why is this act important? What does it represent? (Review the Prologue of *A Home in the Wilderness* where Alsoomse explains the importance of wampum belts, if you need a hint.)

9. Other items are often exchanged during these peace negotiations. What items were exchanged during these peace agreements and renewals? Read through the first part of chapter 28 in the novel. What items were exchanged in that agreement?

10. What if anything surprises you in these documents? What stood out to you as important or interesting?

Name _____

Class _____

Date _____

Discussion Questions Chapter 22

Student Instructions: On the back of this page or a separate sheet of answer the following questions. Be prepared to discuss them with the class. Make sure to put your full name and the date at the top of your answer page.

12. Look up the term "indentured servitude" in a dictionary and write down what you find.

13. Why do you think Etienne's father want to avoid becoming indentured? What would it mean for his family?

14. How does Etienne's father propose to come up with the money the family needs? What plan does Etienne devise?

15. Can you think of any other ways that Etienne and his father could raise the money to pay their debt?

64

Name _____

Class _____

Date _____

Discussion Questions Chapters 23-24

Student Instructions: On the back of this page or a separate sheet of answer the following questions. Be prepared to discuss them with the class.

1. Fire is used for different purposes throughout this story. The author also uses it for foreshadowing and gives it symbolic meanings. Review the Prologue, chapter 1, the last part of chapter 5, and chapters 14, 15, 23 and 24.

2. What does the fire symbolize in the Prologue? Support your answer with evidence from the text.

3. What other meanings does the fire represent? Support your answer with specific evidence and be sure to reference each chapter or page number.

4. Where does the author use fire as a foreshadowing of events to come? Explain your answer.

5. At the end of chapter 25, how does Jean demonstrate his remorse and repentance for his role in the tragedy?

6. A trial jury was held to convict the men who burned the village. What was the makeup of the jury? There are several examples of juries of this nature occurring throughout the early colonies. Why is it important? What legal principal does it represent?

Name _____

Class _____

Date _____

Discussion Questions Chapters 25-27

Student Instructions: On the back of this page or on a separate sheet, answer the following questions. Be prepared to discuss them with the class. Make sure to put your full name and the date at the top of your answer page.

1. Dugout canoes were known to be very valuable to colonists and they often cost as much as a house. Why were dugout canoes so expensive? Why were dugout canoes more desirable than the plank wood rowboats the colonists made?

2. Clock towers had been around since the Middle Ages, but grandfather clocks, the tall standing clocks with pendulums, were only invented in 1656 by Christian Huygens, making them still rare and expensive. What methods did people use for telling time before clock towers? List as many methods as you can.

3. Christian monks were the first European clockmakers, creating the first recorded clock for the future Pope Sylvester II around the year 996. Why do you think it was important for people to keep track of time? Would different professions have different reasons for knowing the time? For example, why did monks need to know the time? Why did sailors need to keep track of the time? Why might farmers need to know the time? Which profession do you think would need the most accurate timepiece? Why?

66

Name _____

Class _____

Date _____

Teacher's Section!!

Completeness _____

Comprehension_____

Clarity/Legibility_____

Total Score: _____

Discussion Questions Chapter 28 and Epilogue

Student Instructions: On the back of this page or a separate sheet of answer the following questions. Be prepared to discuss them with the class. Make sure to put your full name and the date at the top of your answer page.

1. How has Alsoomse's character grown or evolved throughout this story? Support your answer with evidence from the story.

2. Noshi changes in the way he relates to his daughter, especially in how he tolerates her non-traditional behaviors. What might explain the change? Support your answer with specific evidence.

3. How do Alsoomse's non-traditional talents aid her tribe in chapter 23? Do you think this will change how her mother sees her? Why or why not?

4. What method does the author use in the epilogue to introduce a new character? Do you think it is effective? Why or why not?

Name _____

Class _____

Date _____

Essay Prompt

Continuity and Change Over Time

Student Instructions: Write an essay answering the following prompt. Be prepared to discuss it with the class. Make sure to put your full name and the date at the top of your answer page.

Continuity refers to factors that have stayed the same over a long period of time. Using information from the novel, your research on Native American tribes (and notes from other classmates' presentations, if applicable), and any appropriate prior knowledge, answer the following question. Include an arguable thesis statement and be sure to support your answer with specific evidence.

How had relationships among and between Native American tribes changed in terms of culture, economic, political, or social conditions from before Europeans arrive in North America to after various European groups colonized the area. In what ways had these relationships stayed the same?

A Historical Understanding of Time

How people have viewed the concept of time has varied in different regions around the globe and has developed over time with new and more precise methods of measurement.

Many ancient cultures have viewed time as cyclical, meaning that time follows a pattern where natural and human events are repeated in a predictable way. The most famous example of this is the Mayan calendar system, which consists of four different calendars, the smaller time periods rotating within in the larger calendars like gears.[37]

The shortest Mayan calendar was the sacred or ritual calendar, which formed a cycle of 260 days and marked named days for festivals and ceremonies. This calendar rotated inside the solar calendar which lasted 365 days and accounted for leap years in every fourth annum. This calendar then rotated inside the larger "Calendar Round," is made from the interweaving of the first two calendars, which will form a non-repeating pattern lasting 52 years or 18,980 days.[38]

Finally, "Long Count" calendar is a system that counts five cycles of time lasting thousands of years. For example, the previous long count calendar began with creation when the sun was at its zenith on August 11, 3114 B.C. and ended at the winter solstice on December 20, 2012. This largest calendar predicted catastrophic natural events, wars, and other notable phenomena.[39]

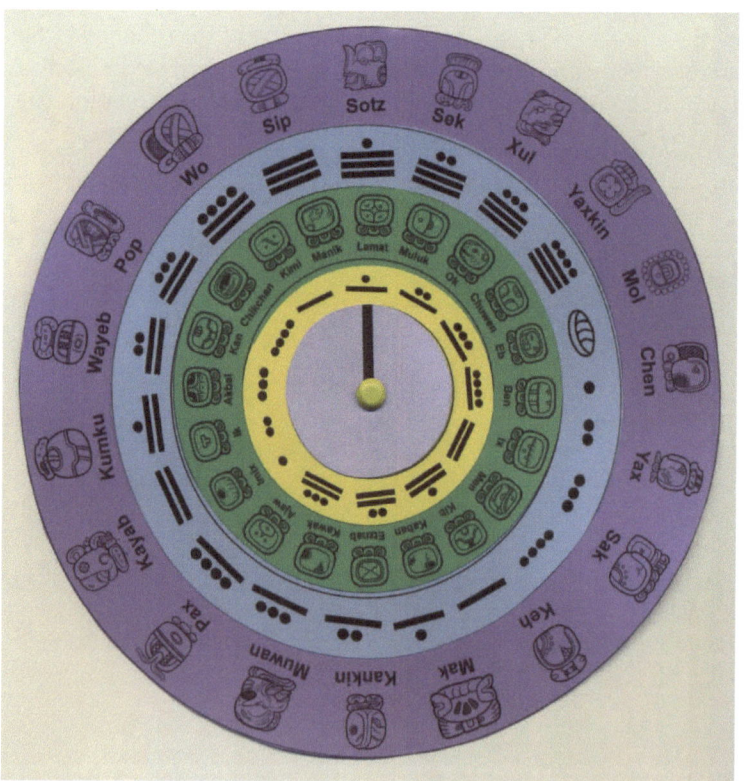

Mayan Calendar System shown in construction paper

---

[37] "The Calendar System," *Living Maya Time*. The Smithsonian National Museum of the American Indians. Accessed September 9, 2024.

In Hindu philosophy time is depicted a wheel called, Kalachakra" or "Wheel of Time." In this belief the universe undergoes endless cycles of creation, preservation, and destruction.[40]

Likewise, the Chinese also believed in a cyclical concept of time associated with astronomical observations and religious rituals. The Shang Dynasty developed a complex calendar system of repeating cycles of "Heavenly Stems," or 10-cycle, and "Earthly Branches," or 12-cycle, which rotate together like gears to create a 10-cycle, called "ganzhi."[41]

The 10-cycle pairs with the early Chinese week. The 12-cycle may have developed into the well-known list of animals used in making predictions. The 60-cycle corresponded to a cycle of 60 years that sought to correlate the solar and lunar cycles from the perspective of the earth.[42]

The Chinese Sexagenary Cycle and the Ritual Foundations of the Calendar

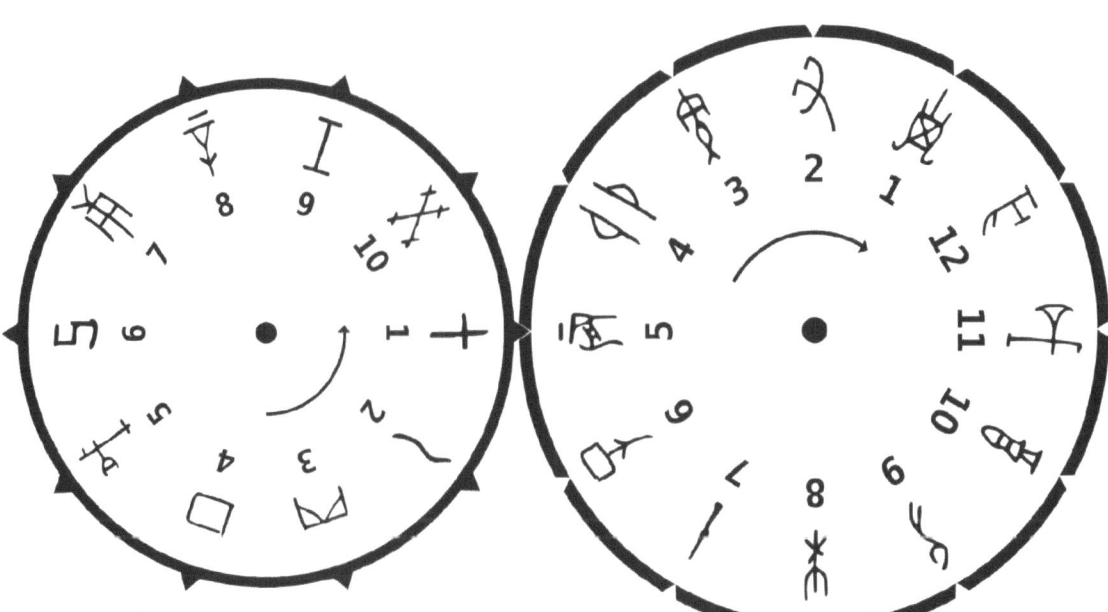

The Chinese Sexagenary Cycle and the Ritual Foundations of the Calendar.

[38] Andrew Evans. "Traveling to the End of the World," *National Geographic*, February 9, 2012. Accessed September 7, 2024.
[39] "The Calendar System," *Living Maya Time.*
[40] John Newman, Geshe Lhundub Sopa (ed.). *The Wheel of Time: Kalachakra in Context.* Shambhala. pp. 51–54, 62–77, 1991.
[41] "Heavenly Stems and Earthly Branches," *Hong Kong Observatory.* Accessed September 9, 2024.
[42] John M. Steele, ed. "The Chinese Sexagenary Cycle and Ritual Origins of the Calendar," in *Calendars and Years II: Astronomy and Time in the Ancient and Medieval World.* Oxford: Oxbow Books, 2010.

In contrast the Abrahamic religions of Judaism, Christianity, and Islam view time as linear, beginning with an act of creation by God and continuing indefinitely.

Jewish and Islamic calendars are based on the lunar calendar of 354 days of twelve synodic months (cycles of the lunar phases). Our modern calendar is based on the amount of time it takes for the Earth to orbit the sun. It takes 356 days, 5 hours, 48 minutes, and 56 seconds for the Earth to complete one orbit. And so, our modern calendar is 356 days long with and extra day every four years (leap year) to adjust for the difference.[43] This explains why the Jewish holiday of Passover and the Islamic observance of Ramadan occur on different days of our modern Gregorian calendar reach year.

The Christian calendar is laid out in a timeline marking the birth of Jesus Christ roughly in the center. Anything prior to Christ's birth is referenced as B.C. or "before Christ." Everything after Christ's birth is designated as A.D. or "Anno Domini" (Latin for "in the year of our Lord"). In recent years, these notations have been replaced with BCE (before current era) and CE (current era) to secularize the notations or remove the Christian references.

Easter is the major holiday in Christianity which commemorates when Jesus Christ was crucified (or executed) by the Romans, was buried, and then rose from the dead after three days on Easter Sunday. After spending several days with his disciples (now known as the Apostles) Christ ascended into heaven. Christian theology then references the "End Times" as those events that will occur after Christ returns to earth.

Question: *Why does the Christian timeline mix English and Latin references in the notation of B.C. and A.D.?*

In the early Middle Ages, years were recorded in reference to the year of the reigning Roman emperor. After Christianity became the dominant religion in the Mediterranean region, the celebration of Easter became an important driving factor in the study of mathematics. The First Council of Nicaea, in A.D. 325, had decided that Easter would follow the spring equinox.

But it wasn't until A.D. 525 when a monk named Dionysius Exiguus introduced the A.D. system by counting backwards to the year of Christ's birth, according to Georges Declercq, a history teacher at Vrije Universiteit Brussel in an article published in the Journal Sacris Erudiri in 2002.

Apparently, Dionysius devised the system to replace the Diocletian system, which was named after the emperor who had martyred many Christians. He was off in his calculations though, because it is now believed by most Biblical scholars that Jesus was born in 4 or 6 A.D.

The addition of the B.C. component came two centuries later when the Venerable Bede of Northumbria published his book the "Ecclesiastical History of the English People" in 731. He expanded the A.D. system to include prior years, numbering them to count backward to indicate the number of years an event had occurred "before Christ" was born.

(Information obtained from Robert Coolman and Owen Jarus, "Keeping Time: The origin of B.C. and A.D.", January 14, 2022. Accessed September 9, 2024)

---

[43] Bob Craddock, "The Science of Leap Year," *National Air and Space Museum.* Smithsonian. February 27, 2020. Accessed September 10, 2024.

The Development of Clocks Timeline*

3,500 B.C.   **Obelisks** were used in ancient Egypt and are among the earliest shadow clocks.

Egyptian Obelisk, Image taken by Ahmed M. Hanfy, April 14, 2018.
Creative Commons Attribution-Share Alike 4.0 International

2,000 B.C.   **Base-60-time system** is the use of a 60-minute and 60-second increment clock dates to ancient Sumeria.

1,500 B.C.   **Sundials** were developed to measure the parts of the day.

Replica of a Roman sundial (scaphe), by Manfred Heyde, September 2008. Public Domain.

520 B.C.   **Candle clocks** were first mentioned in a Chinese poem describing a graduated candle that burned at a measured rate. These were used for determining the time at night. They were also used in Japan.

325 B.C.   **Water clocks**, called a clepsydra, were invented by the Greeks in which rising waters fed ofrom a stream or aqueduct kept track of the time. A face with a dial measured off the hours. They were useful because they could be used indoors, at night, or in cloudy weather.

996 A.D.   **Monastery clocks and clock towers** were used to call people to prayer. The first mechanical clock was bult by the future Pope Sylvester II. They used weights to slowly move the hour hand.

1400s A.D.   **Hourglasses** were the first dependable and reasonably accurate time-measurement devise. They were primarily used at sea, but were also adopted for use in churches, industry, and cooking.

1504   **Pendant and pocket watches**. The first portable timepiece was invented by Peter Henlein in Nuremberg, Germany, but it was not very accurate.

Fun Fact: French mathematician and philosopher, Blaise Pascal (1623-1662), was the first reported person to wear a wristwatch, by using a piece of string to attach his pocket watch to his wrist.

1577   **The Minute hand** was invented by Jost Burgi in a clock he made for Tycho Brahe, an astronomer who needed an accurate clock for tracking the stars.

1656   **The pendulum clock** was invented by Christian Huygens.

1876   **A Mechanical wind-up clock** was patented by Seth E. Thomas.

Fun Fact: American inventor Levi Hutchinson of Concord, New Hampshire created the first mechanical alarm clock in 1787. However, the ringing bell alarm on his clock could only ring at 4:00 in the morning!

1878   **Standard time** was invented by Sir Sanford Fleming to synchronize all clocks within a geographical region into a single time standard to facilitate weather forecasting and time travel. Time zones were not created until the 20th century.

1912   **Battery-powered clocks** were produced by the newly formed Westclox Clock Company. Previously clocks were either wound by hand or run by weights.

1923   **Self-winding watches** were invented by John Harwood.

1927   **The quartz clock** was invented by Canadian-born Warren Marrison, a telecommunications engineer at Bell Telephone Laboratories, in his search for reliable frequency standards. It is a highly accurate clock based on the regular vibrations of a quartz crystal in an electric current.

Historical Understanding of Time and the Development of Clocks
Discussion Questions

Student Instructions: On the back of this page or a separate sheet of answer the following questions. Be prepared to discuss them with the class.

1. How did the Mayan understanding of time and the creation of their calendar compare with that of the Shang Dynasty in China? How were they different?

2. Why do you think humans have been concerned with measuring time? What purposes does it serve? Did different socio-economic groups have different reasons for wanting to measure time? For example, did kings or priests have a different reason for calendars than peasants? Why or why not? Be specific in your answer and give examples to support your argument.

3. Think about how ancient people measured time and compare it to how we measure time today. (Hint: Think about our calendars and the development of clocks.) What similarities can you find? What is different? What might explain the differences. Be specific.

4. In what way is the Abrahamic understanding of time different from the other systems discussed earlier? How do you think these differences would affect the myths or beliefs these different cultures held? Explain your answer.

5. Hindu religion believes that when people die their souls can be reincarnated, or reborn, into new bodies. How does this belief fit with the ancient Hindu understanding of time? Explain your answer.

74

6. Christianity grew out of Judaism. In the Hebrew Bible (the Old Testament in Christian Bibles) the Israelites were told to watch for a messiah (Mashiah, "anointed") from the descendants of King David, who would come and deliver Israel from foreign bondage and restore the glorious golden age.

Christianity then believes that Jesus was the promised Messiah, though believers claim that he came to save not just the Israelites, but also all humans, and not from a physical domination by foreign power (the Roman Empire), but from a spiritual domination from evil, or sin. Christian doctrine (belief) says that the only way for Jesus to do this was to die as the perfect sacrifice for the sins of the world. Jesus could do this because he was not only a man, but he was also God, and therefore he was perfect, without sin as God is. But he would not be dominated by death because he would be resurrected (become alive again) after three days and have victory even over death and for all time.

Review the information provided above regarding Easter and the "End Times."

How does Christian belief require a linear understanding of time (rather than a cyclical understanding)? Explain your answer.

Individual/Group Project

Create a Sundial

What You Will Need:

- 1 paper plate (or a circle cut out of cardstock or cardboard)

- 1 chopstick stick (or pencil, popsicle stick, or straw)

- 1 pointed object (scissors, or sharpened pencil)

- Markers

- Watch

- Compass (optional)

Materials needed, ©Windy Sea Publishing, 2024.

Preparation:

23. Find the center of the paper plate, and carefully cut a small hole or slit for the chopstick (or pencil, chopstick, or straw). If you don't have a paper plate, you can cut an 8-inch circle from cardboard or cardstock.

24. Place the chopstick or pencil in the hole or slit you made.

25. Write the number 12 at the top edge of the plate. This will represent noon.

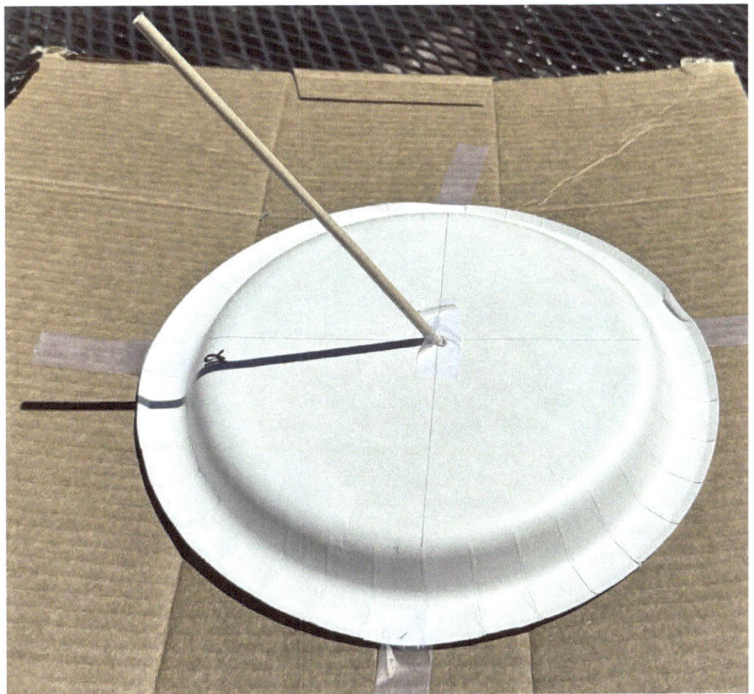

Sundial model, ©Windy Sea Publishing, 2024.

Procedure:

1. Find a sunny, open place in your yard and place your sundial on the ground just before 12:00 noon. Rotate the plate so that the shadow from your popsicle or pencil lines up with the number 12 as the clock reaches 12:00.

2. Using a compass locate the direction North and slightly angle your popsicle or pencil in the direction of north. If you don't have a compass, angle the popsicle in the direction of the shadow.

3. Do not move your sundial. You many need to place a few rocks on it to hold it in place.

4. Come back at 1:00 and write the number 1 in the place where the shadow hits the edge of the plate. You can also use a ruler to draw a line along the shadow as the ancients did. You may want to set a timer so that you won't forget!

5. Repeat this process every hour, increasing the number by one for every hour until the sun sets.

6. If it is not going to rain, and you can leave the sundial in place over night, you can get up in the morning and complete the sundial to count each morning hour.

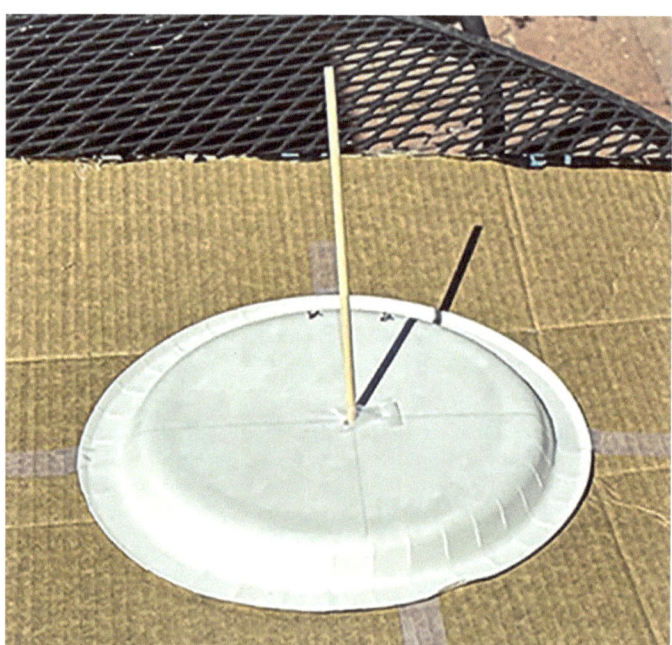

Sundial procedure. ©Windy Sea Publishing.

Answer the following Questions:

7. Why does the shadow move throughout the day?

8. Did the length of the shadows stay the same or change? If they changed, how did they change? Why do you think they changed?

Experiment Extension:

Test to see whether your sundial will still work to predict the time at different times of the year.

Was your prediction correct? Why or why not?

Note to Teachers:

A sundial tracks the apparent movement of the sun as the Earth rotates on its axis. The length of the shadow made by the vertical object, called a "gnoman," as it crosses the dial surface is caused by the tilt of the Earth in relation to the sun during different times of the year. For example, in the summer in the northern hemispher the sun is higher in the sky and will create a shorter shadow. But in the winter when the sun is lower in the sky the shadow will be longer.

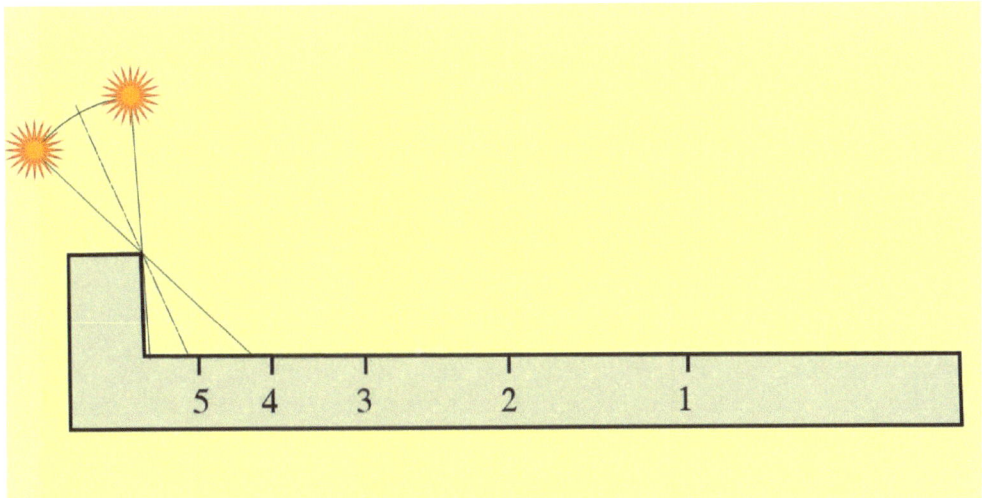

"Projections of the shadow of the Sun, at noon, at the solstices, in Luxor," diagram by Aubry Gérard. Creative Commons Attribution-Share Alike 4.0 License

"The Sinnington sundial," photo by Pauline E. Creative Commons Attribution-Share Alike 2.0.

Essay Prompt

Wrap-up Essay Ideas

Student Instructions: Choose one of the following essay prompts, and write an essay answering your chosen prompt.

1. Why did different groups of European settlers come to North America? What were they hoping to achieve? Support your answer with specific evidence.

2. Based on what you have learned in these lessons, what kind of a relationship did many of European settlers hope to have with the Native American tribes? Were they able to achieve these goals? Why or why not? Support your answer with specific evidence.

3. Based on what you have learned in these lessons, what kind of a relationship did many of the Native American tribes want to have with the European settlers? Were they able to achieve these goals? Why or why not? Support your answer with specific evidence.

4. Was it inevitable that the European settlers and the Native American tribes would experience conflict between and among the different groups? Explain your answer with specific evidence.

5. Think back to your studies from World History, how do the conflicts between the European colonists and the Native American tribes compare to other conflicts you have studied? In what ways are both conflicts similar? In what ways are they different?

6. Thinking about the conflicts you have studied in this unit and others you have studied, in general terms (big picture), why do different groups of people get into conflicts? Support your answer with at least three to four specific examples from different regions/conflicts.

7. Pretend that you are a negotiator, and it is your job to help the Dutch colonists and the Esopus people resolve their differences peaceably. How would you help them solve this conflict? What would you say to each group to help them to reach a compromise? What would each side have to give up in order to reach a compromise? What would each side gain from the compromise?

8. Conflict can be resolved through the utter defeat of one side by another, or through compromise. Given the destruction that often comes from a total defeat, why is it so difficult for groups of people to agree to compromise? Now think about a current conflict (political, social, or economic) that is going on in your country today. What do you think would have to happen in order for both sides to agree to a compromise?

Name _____

Class _____

Date _____

Wrap-Up Book Projects

Student Instructions: As a group, choose one of the following project ideas and work together to create the project, answer the questions, and create a presentation.

1. Propaganda Poster

   Materials:
   - Poster board
   - Crayons, markers, and/or colored pencils

   Instructions:
   - On one side of the poster, create a graphic image that will appeal to an audience and entice them want to move to the New World. Conversely, you could create a poster to rally other tribes to join yours in fighting against the invading Europeans. Use symbolism and color to covey your message with as few words as possible.
   - On the other side, answer the following questions:
     a. What is your poster trying to get others to do?
     b. Why did you choose/create/design this image?
     c. Explain your use of symbolism and color. What do the various images mean? Do the colors you chose have a particular meaning? If so, what does it mean? Or if you used color to highlight certain aspects, what message were you trying to convey.

2. Documentary Trailer

   Materials:
   - Video camera or phone
   - iMovie or other digital movie-making software. Files should be formatted in mp4.

   Instructions:
   - Create a 3-5 minute movie trailer either for a movie adaptation of the book or for a documentary about the colony of New Netherlands. Choose and include at least 6 scenes from the book or documentary. For each scene create a:
     a. Video clip of the scene reenactment or an "expert" discussing a theme or important event. Do not show the entire scene, interview, or monologue, only enough to convey the essential conclusion or enticement. Remember you are trying to convince someone to watch the full movie or documentary and convey an overall thesis.
     b. A written explanation of why you chose to include each scene in your trailer and what conclusion you are trying to convey.

3. Recreation exhibit

   Materials:
   - Wooden board or stiff cardboard base
   - Something to make figurines or settlements, and other landscape elements
     Modeling clay

Popsicle sticks and paper

Legos

Etc.

Instructions:

- Create a bird's-eye view of a 3-Dimensional replica of an important scene from the novel.
- On a separate sheet of paper answer the following questions:
    a. What scene did you choose? Provide a paragraph summary of the scene you chose to display.
    b. In what stage of the novel is this portrayed?
        o Exposition
        o Inciting Incident
        o Rising Action
        o Climax
        o Resolution
    c. Why did you choose this scene? Why do you consider this scene important to the novel?

4. Persuasive Letter

Materials:

- Paper and Pen or Computer/Laptop

Instructions:

- Imagine that a school is considering adding this book to their English Language Arts curriculum. Write a persuasive letter to the school board explaining why you would or would not recommend this book for their curriculum.
- The essay should be AT LEAST five paragraphs including an introductory paragraph and a concluding paragraph.
- Make sure to plan out your argument, listing reasons you would recommend it and reasons you would not recommend it. You should include both even if your argument is for one or the other. You will include this organizer with the essay.
- Make sure to textual evidence to support your argument.

5. Interview One or More Characters

Materials:

- Costumes and Props for characters
- Set pieces (chairs, tables, tablecloths, etc.)
- Optional: May be filmed ahead of time and presented as a mp4.

Instructions:

- Your group will be acting out a character interview. One person in the group will be the interviewer and the others will each play the role of a character.
- Create a script of questions (for the interviewer) and answers (for the characters). This script should include at least 5 open-ended questions for each character being interviewed. These questions should require more than one-word answers.
- With your script, you should also include a short explanation of why you chose to interview each character.
- As you act out the interview, make sure either to memorize your lines or that everyone has their own copy of the script and to try to speak and act like the character you are portraying.
- Interview should not exceed 10 minutes.

Appendix A
Checklists and Rubrics

Name: _____   Class: _____   Date: _____

Checklist for Evaluating Sources

Use the following checklist to evaluate the reliability of the source material:

Author, Editor, or Creator:

_____   Did a reliable person or organization create this document?

_____   Is the author, editor, or creator an expert on the topic?

_____   Can you confirm the credentials of the source?

Content:

_____   Is the information based on fact or opinion?

_____   Is the content balanced, addressing multiple points of view, or one-sided?
(If the source has a particular bias, be sure to balance it out with sources of opposing perspectives.)

_____   Is the information complete and accurate, compared to other sources read?

_____   What is the point of view of the source? How objective is it?
(Check for use of emotional words, exaggerations, direct promotion of a specific view.)

Context:

_____   What is the purpose of the document? Is it meant to educate or persuade?

_____   How have the major events or beliefs from the time the source was written or produced influenced this document?

_____   Does the information cite other reliable sources?

Name: _____   Class: _____   Date: _____

Discussion Question Rubric

Weight	Category	Incomplete 1	Minimally Proficient 2	Partially Proficient 3	Proficient 4	Highly Proficient 5
x1	Completeness Standards: 8.RI/RL.10; 8.L.6	Student has failed to answer many of the questions, has missed most parts of the questions, and/or has written one word or one sentence responses.	Student has answered some of the questions but not all or student has missed parts of some of the questions. Student has missed several key elements or themes in their answers. Student might have only written a sentence or two for each paragraph.	Student has answered all parts of all the questions, but answers do not fully explore the topic. Student might have missed a key element or theme in their answer. Student has written at least a short paragraph for each response.	All responses are thorough and answer all parts of all the questions. Student has written at least a complete paragraph for each response.	All responses are thorough and answer all parts of all the questions, even going above and beyond, adding insight not directly asked for. Student has written more than a complete paragraph for each response.
x3	Comprehension Standards: 8.RI/RL.1-3, 5, 6, 9	Student displays minimal or no understanding of the topic/central idea, text structure, author point of view and/or literary/technical elements of the text. Student does not use evidence to support their explanation.	Student displays some understanding of the topic/central idea, text structure, author point of view and/or literary/technical elements of the text. Student uses evidence, but it may be confusing or disconnected from their analysis.	Student displays a basic understanding of the topic/central idea, text structure, author point of view and/or literary/technical elements of the text. Student uses evidence, but it may not be the strongest example and/or may not clearly connect to their analysis.	All responses display a complete understanding of the topic/central idea, text structure, author point of view and/or literary/technical elements of the text. Student uses relevant evidence and connects it to their analysis.	All responses display a complete, complex and insightful understanding of the topic/central idea, text structure, author point of view and/or literary/technical elements of the text. Student chooses strong and relevant evidence and clearly connects it to their analysis.
x1	Clarity/Legibility Standards: 8.RI/RL.4; 8.L.1-5	Student's text is barely legible due to many grammar and spelling mistakes.	Student has several grammar or spelling mistakes.	Student uses correct grammar and spelling.	Student uses correct grammar and spelling, choosing appropriate, interesting language (including any technical terminology from the text) to add variety to the text.	Student uses correct grammar and spelling. Student chooses appropriate, interesting language (including any technical terminology from the text) and factors in connotation and context in order to add variety, precision, and conciseness to the text.

Teacher Comments:

Name: _____   Class: _____   Date: _____

Discussion Question and Annotation Rubric

Weight	Category	Incomplete 1	Minimally Proficient 2	Partially Proficient 3	Proficient 4	Highly Proficient 5
x1	Completeness Standards: 8.RI.10; 8.L.6	Student has failed to answer many of the questions, has missed most parts of the questions, and/or has written one word or one sentence responses. Student has not put any effort into completing their annotation guide.	Student has answered some of the questions but not all or student has missed parts of some of the questions. Student has missed several key elements or themes in their answers. Student might have only written a sentence or two for each paragraph. Student is missing many elements in their annotation guide.	Student has answered all parts of all the questions, but answers do not fully explore the topic. Student might have missed a key element or theme in their answer. Student has written at least a short paragraph for each response. Student is some key elements in their annotation guide.	All responses are thorough and answer all parts of all the questions. Student has written at least a complete paragraph for each response. Student has completed all parts of their annotations guide.	All responses are thorough and answer all parts of all the questions, even going above and beyond, adding insight not directly asked for. Student has written more than a complete paragraph for each response. Student has completed all parts of annotation guide and provided additional insight in their comments and answers.
x3	Comprehension Standards: 8.RI.1-3, 5, 6	Student displays minimal or no understanding of the topic/central idea, text structure, author point of view and/or literary/technical elements of the text. Student does not use evidence to support their explanation.	Student displays some understanding of the topic/central idea, text structure, author point of view and/or literary/technical elements of the text. Student uses evidence, but it may be confusing or disconnected from their analysis.	Student displays a basic understanding of the topic/central idea, text structure, author point of view and/or literary/technical elements of the text. Student uses evidence, but it may not be the strongest example and/or may not clearly connect to their analysis.	All responses display a complete understanding of the topic/central idea, text structure, author point of view and/or literary/technical elements of the text. Student uses relevant evidence and connects it to their analysis.	All responses display a complete, complex, and insightful understanding of the topic/central idea, text structure, author point of view, and/or literary/technical elements of the text. Student chooses clear, strong, and relevant evidence and clearly connects it to their analysis.
x1	Clarity/Legibility Standards: 8.RI.4; 8.L.1-5	Student's text is barely legible due to many grammar and spelling mistakes.	Student has several grammar or spelling mistakes.	Student uses correct grammar and spelling.	Student uses correct grammar and spelling, choosing appropriate, interesting language (including any technical terminology from the text) to add variety to the text.	Student uses correct grammar & spelling. Student chooses appropriate, interesting language (including any technical terminology from the text) and factors in connotation and context in order to add variety, precision, and conciseness to the text.

Teacher Comments:

Name: _____ Class: _____ Date: _____

Argumentative Essay Rubric

Weight	Category	Incomplete 1	Minimally Proficient 2	Partially Proficient 3	Proficient 4	Highly Proficient 5
x1	Claim Standards: 8.W.1a, 4	The student does not have a clear or arguable claim.	Student makes a claim, but it may be hard to identify and/or not in the introduction. Student does not acknowledge alternate or opposing claims. Few points, arguments, or evidence points back to the claim.	Student makes an arguable claim in the introduction. Student tries to acknowledge alternate or opposing claims but may not do so accurately or fairly. Throughout the essay, most points, arguments, and evidence point back to the claim.	Student makes an arguable claim in the introduction. Student also acknowledges and refutes alternate or opposing claims. Throughout the essay, all points, arguments, and evidence point back to the claim.	Student makes a clear, solid, and arguable claim in the introduction. Student also acknowledges and effectively refutes alternate or opposing claims. Throughout the essay, all points, arguments, and evidence clearly point back to the claim.
x2	Evidence Standards: 8.W.1b, 4	Claims presented are not supported with evidence.	Not all claims presented are supported with evidence. Evidence comes from sources that may or may not be credible or accurate and/or may not be correctly cited.	All claims presented are supported with evidence or logical reasoning. Evidence comes from accurate and credible sources but may not be correctly cited.	All claims presented are supported with relevant evidence and logical reasoning. Evidence comes from accurate and credible sources and is correctly cited.	All claims presented are supported with clear, strong, and relevant evidence and insightful, logical reasoning. Evidence comes from accurate, credible, and interesting sources written by experts and is correctly cited.
x1	Organization Standards: 8.W.1c, 1e, 4	The essay has no clear structure or transitions between ideas.	Student includes an introduction, body, and conclusion in the essay but doesn't write complete paragraphs or sentences. The introduction may not include a claim while the conclusion may only consist of a generalities or filler sentences.	Student includes an introduction, body, and conclusion in the essay. The introduction includes a claim while the conclusion attempts to wrap up the argument by simply rephrasing or repeating the claim. Student attempts to use transition words, phrases, or clauses but essay might still feel choppy.	Student includes a clear introduction, body, and conclusion in the essay. The introduction includes an interesting hook and clear claim while the conclusion neatly wraps up and supports the argument. Student uses transition words, phrases, or clauses to create a cohesive argument.	Student includes a clear introduction, body, and conclusion in the essay. The introduction includes an interesting hook and clear, concise claim while the conclusion neatly wraps up and supports the argument while adding a new and insightful way to look at the claim. Student creatively uses vivid and interesting transition words, phrases, or clauses to create a fluid, cohesive argument.
x1	Language Standards: 8.W.1d, 4; 8.L.1-3	Student's text is barely legible due to many grammar and spelling mistakes. Student fails to maintain a formal style.	Student has several grammar or spelling mistakes. Student attempts a formal style but still has several slang terms or personal pronouns.	Student uses correct grammar and spelling. Student mostly maintains a formal style throughout the text removing most slang and personal pronouns but might have missed a few.	Student uses correct grammar and spelling, choosing appropriate, interesting language (including any technical terminology from the text) to add variety to the text. Student maintains a formal style throughout the text, removing all slang and personal pronouns.	Student uses correct grammar and spelling. Student chooses appropriate, interesting language (including any technical terminology from the text) and factors in connotation and context in order to add variety, precision, and conciseness to the text. Student maintains a formal style throughout the text, removing all slang and personal pronouns.

Teacher Comments:

Name: _____   Class: _____   Date: _____

Informative Essay Rubric

Weight	Category	Incomplete 1	Minimally Proficient 2	Partially Proficient 3	Proficient 4	Highly Proficient 5
x1	Topic Standards: 8.W.2a, 4	The student does not have a clear topic/central idea nor any strategies to convey information. The essay reads like a confusing ramble.	Student attempts to introduce the topic/central idea but it is not specific or clear enough. Student attempts to use a strategy to convey information but does not make clear connections to the topic.	Student introduces the topic/central idea but may not include a preview of the essay. Student uses at least one strategy, such as definitions, classifications, comparisons/contrasts, or cause and effect to organize and convey information.	Student introduces the topic/central idea and a brief preview of the essay in the introduction. Student uses some combinations of strategies such as definitions, classifications, comparisons/contrasts, and/or cause and effect to organize and convey ideas, concepts, and information.	Student introduces the topic/central idea and a brief preview of the essay clearly and concisely in the introduction. Student uses many strategies such as definitions, classifications, comparisons/contrasts, and cause and effect to organize and effectively convey ideas, concepts, and information.
x2	Evidence Standards: 8.W.2b, 4	Claims presented are not supported with evidence.	Not all claims presented are supported with evidence. Evidence comes from sources that may or may not be credible or accurate and/or may not be correctly cited.	All claims presented are supported with evidence, including relevant facts, definitions, concrete details, or quotations. Evidence comes from accurate and credible sources but may not be correctly cited.	All claims presented are supported with relevant evidence, including some combination of relevant facts, definitions, concrete details, and/or quotations. Evidence comes from accurate and credible sources and is correctly cited.	All claims presented are supported with clear, strong, relevant evidence, including relevant facts, definitions, concrete details, and quotations. Evidence comes from accurate, credible, and interesting sources written by experts & is correctly cited.
x1	Organization Standards: 8.W.2c, 2f, 4	The essay has no clear structure or transitions between ideas.	Student includes an introduction, body, and conclusion in the essay but doesn't write complete paragraphs or sentences. The introduction may not include a claim while the conclusion may only consist of generalities or filler sentences.	Student includes an introduction, body, and conclusion in the essay. The introduction includes a claim while the conclusion attempts to wrap up the essay by simply rephrasing or repeating the claim. Student attempts to use transition words, phrases, or clauses but essay might still feel choppy.	Student includes a clear introduction, body, and conclusion in the essay. The introduction includes an interesting hook and clear claim while the conclusion neatly wraps up and supports the essay. Student uses transition words, phrases, or clauses to create a cohesive argument.	Student includes a clear introduction, body, and conclusion in the essay. The introduction includes an interesting hook and clear, concise claim while the conclusion neatly wraps up and supports the essay while adding a new and insightful way to look at the claim. Student creatively uses vivid and interesting transition words, phrases, or clauses to create a fluid, cohesive argument.
x1	Language Standards: 8.W.2d, 2e, 4; 8.L.1-3	Student's text is barely legible due to many grammar and spelling mistakes. Student fails to maintain a formal style.	Student has several grammar or spelling mistakes. Student attempts a formal style but still has several slang terms or personal pronouns.	Student uses correct grammar and spelling. Student mostly maintains a formal style throughout the text removing most slang and personal pronouns but might have missed a few.	Student uses correct grammar and spelling, choosing appropriate, interesting language (including any technical terminology from the text) to add variety to the text. Student maintains a formal style throughout the text, removing all slang and personal pronouns.	Student uses correct grammar and spelling. Student chooses appropriate, interesting language (including any technical terminology from the text) & factors in connotation & context in order to add variety, precision, & conciseness to the text. Student maintains a formal style throughout the text, removing all slang and personal pronouns.

Name: _____ Class: _____ Date: _____

Narrative Essay Rubric

Weight	Category	Incomplete 1	Minimally Proficient 2	Partially Proficient 3	Proficient 4	Highly Proficient 5
x1	Introduction Standards: 8.W.3a, 4	Student does not orient the reader or establish context.	Student attempts to orient the reader by establishing a context, setting, and POV but may have some unnecessary or missing details. Story progression feels choppy or unbelievable.	Student orients the reader by establishing a context, setting, and POV. Story progresses mostly believably from the introduction.	Student engages and orients the reader with an interesting opening line and quickly establishes a context, setting, and POV. Story progresses believably from the introduction.	Student engages and orients the reader with a captivating opening line and quickly and effectively establishes a context, setting, and POV. Story progresses naturally, surprisingly, and believably from the introduction.
x2	Narrative Standards: 8.W.3b, 4	Student does not use narrative techniques and/or they do not develop the story at all	Student uses few narrative techniques, such as dialogue, acing, and sensory descriptions, and/or they do not fully develop setting, character, or events.	Student uses some narrative techniques, such as dialogue, pacing, and sensory descriptions, to develop setting, events, and characters.	Student uses narrative techniques, such as dialogue, pacing, and sensory descriptions, to develop setting, events, and characters.	Student uses narrative techniques, such as interesting dialogue, exciting pacing, and vivid, sensory descriptions, to develop immersive settings, engaging events, and relatable characters.
x1	Organization Standards: 8.W.3c, 3e, 4	The story has no clear structure or transitions between events and the story is confusing and/or does not include an introduction or conclusion.	Student includes an introduction, body, and conclusion in the story. The introduction may include a hook but does not have enough exposition to establish the story while the conclusion may not believably flow from the events of the story and/or the student may have rushed through the story, skipping important scenes. Student does not use many transitions.	Student includes an introduction, body, and conclusion in the story. The introduction includes a hook and some exposition while the conclusion wraps up the story in a way that is mostly believable. Student uses some transition words, phrases, or clauses to create a clear timeframe, setting and sequence of events.	Student includes a clear introduction, body, and conclusion in the story. The introduction includes an interesting hook and exposition while the conclusion neatly wraps up the story in a way that flows both naturally and believably from the events of the story. Student uses interesting transition words, phrases, or clauses to create a cohesive timeframe, setting and sequence of events.	Student includes a clear introduction, body, and conclusion in the story. The introduction includes an interesting hook and exposition while the conclusion neatly wraps up the story in a way that flows both naturally and surprisingly from the events of the story as well as with the characters' goals and motivations. Student creatively uses vivid and interesting transition words, phrases, or clauses to create a fluid, cohesive timeframe, setting and sequence of events.
x1	Language Standards: 8.W.3d, 4; 7.L.1-3	Student's text is barely legible due to many grammar and spelling mistakes.	Student has several grammar or spelling mistakes.	Student uses correct grammar and spelling.	Student uses correct grammar and spelling, choosing appropriate, interesting language (including any technical terminology from the text) to add variety to the text.	Student uses correct grammar and spelling. Student chooses applicable, interesting language (including any technical terminology from the text) and factors in connotation and context in order to add variety, precision, & conciseness to the text.

Teacher Comments:

88

Presentation Rubric

Weight	Category	Incomplete 1	Minimally Proficient 2	Partially Proficient 3	Proficient 4	Highly Proficient 5
x1	Preparation and Collaboration Standards: 8.SL.1a-d	Students do not come to discussions or the presentation prepared. The group squabbles and cannot get along or work together.	Some students come to group discussions prepared and/or the presentation, having read most materials and/or completing assigned tasks. Students attempt open discussion but there are a several heated or ineffective discussions. Students struggle to acknowledge new information or ideas expressed by others and/or struggle to find acceptable compromises. Students struggle to ask questions and/or answer questions posed by others. Students do not attempt to track progress and fall behind in their project.	Most students come to group discussions prepared and the presentation, having read all materials and/or completing assigned tasks. Students are open to discussion but there are a few ineffective or heated discussions. Students acknowledge new information or ideas expressed by others and are able to compromise though some students may still feel left out. Students are able to pose questions and answer questions posed by others. Students attempt to track progress but may miss specific deadlines or may not accomplish all goals.	All students come to all group discussions and the presentation prepared, having read all materials and/or completing assigned tasks. Students are open to discussion but there might be some easily resolved problems. Students acknowledge new information or ideas expressed by others and are able to form acceptable compromises. Students are able to pose questions and answer questions posed by others. Students track progress and keep specific goals and deadlines.	All students come to all group discussions and the presentation prepared, having read all materials and/or completing assigned tasks. Students are open to reasonable discussions without arguments. Students acknowledge new information or ideas expressed by others are able to create solutions/ideas that work for all. Students are able to pose thought-provoking questions and insightfully answer questions posed by others. Students effectively track progress and keep specific goals and deadlines.
x2	Content and Completion Standards: 8.SL.5; 8.L.1-3	Students do not have any visual elements to include.	Students have included visual displays in order to help make their points, but it is unfinished and/or messy and disorganized with many grammar mistakes.	Students have included visual displays in order to help make their points. There are few grammar mistakes made and most of the work has been completed.	Students have included interesting visual displays in order to help make their points. There are no grammar mistakes made and all work has been completed.	Students have included captivating and interesting visual displays in order to help make their points. There are no grammar mistakes made and all work has been completed a with high attention to detail.
x2	Presentation and Articulation Standards: 8.SL.4, 6; 8.L.3	Most or all of the students' claims and ideas are confusing. Most students are off task & unfocused. Students do not make good eye contact/or use an appropriate volume. There are many pronunciation errors and students sound monotone. There is no obvious organization, and no one knows who is supposed to speak.	Some of the students' claims and ideas are confusing. Several students are off task and unfocused. Students struggle to make good eye contact and/or use an appropriate volume. There are many pronunciation errors and students struggle to vary their tone. The presentation is poorly organized and/or the students do not know who is supposed to speak.	Students present their claims, findings, and ideas mostly coherently. Most students are on task and focused. Most students make good eye contact and use an appropriate volume. There are few pronunciation errors and students attempt to vary their tone in order to emphasize their important points. The presentation is mostly organized.	Students present their claims, findings, and ideas coherently. No student is off task or unfocused. Students make strong eye contact and use an appropriate volume. All words are clearly pronounced, and students vary their tone in order to emphasize salient points. The presentation is well organized.	Students present their claims, findings, & ideas coherently and engagingly. No student it off task or unfocused. All students make strong eye contact and use an appropriate volume that can be heard from anywhere in the room. All words are clearly and correctly pronounced, & students vary their tone and speech appropriately for the style of presentation in order to emphasize salient points and/or to create excitement/engagement with their listeners. Presentation is smooth and well organized.

Name: _____   Class: _____   Date: _____

		Research Project Rubric				
Weight	Category	Incomplete 1	Minimally Proficient 2	Partially Proficient 3	Proficient 4	Highly Proficient 5
x1	Research Standards: 8.W.1a, 1b, 2a, 2b, 4-9	The student does not have a clear topic/central idea. Claims presented are not supported with evidence.	Student attempt to introduce the topic/central idea but it is not specific or clear enough. Not all claims presented are supported with evidence. Evidence comes from sources that may or may not be credible or accurate and/or may not be correctly cited.	Student introduces the topic/central idea but may not include a preview of the essay. All claims presented are supported with evidence, including relevant facts, definitions, concrete details, or quotations. Evidence comes from accurate and credible sources but may not be correctly cited.	Student introduces the topic/central idea and a brief preview of the essay in the introduction. All claims presented are supported with relevant evidence, including some combination of facts, definitions, concrete details, and/or quotations. Evidence comes from accurate and credible sources and is correctly cited.	Student introduces the topic/central idea and a brief preview of the essay clearly and concisely in the introduction. All claims presented are supported with clear, strong, and relevant evidence, including facts, definitions, concrete details, and quotations. Evidence comes from accurate, credible, and interesting sources written by experts and is correctly cited.
x2	Analysis Standards: 8.RI/RL.1-3, 5-9; 8.SL.2, 3	Student displays minimal or no understanding of the topic/central idea, text structure, author point of view and/or literary/technical elements of the text. Student cannot find any comparisons or contrasts between the texts and cannot trace the author's arguments. Student does not use evidence to support their explanation.	Student displays some understanding of the topic/central idea, text structure, author point of view and/or literary/technical elements of the text. Student is able to find simple comparisons and contrasts between most of the texts. Student struggles to trace arguments or specific claims in the texts but cannot assess their effectiveness. Student uses evidence, but it may be confusing or disconnected from their analysis.	Student displays a basic understanding of the topic/central idea, text structure, author point of view and/or literary/technical elements of the text. Student is able to find comparisons and contrasts between most of the texts. Student can trace arguments or specific claims in the texts but may struggle to assess their effectiveness. Student uses evidence, but it may not be the strongest example and/or may not clearly connect to their analysis.	All responses display a complete understanding of the topic/central idea, text structure, author point of view and/or literary/technical elements of the text. Student is able to find strong comparisons and contrasts between all the texts. Student can trace and evaluate arguments or specific claims in the texts and assess their effectiveness. Student uses relevant evidence and connects it to their analysis.	All responses display a complete, complex, and insightful understanding of the topics/central ideas, text structures, point of views, and/or literary/technical elements of all the texts. Student is able to find meaningful and insightful comparisons and contrasts between all the texts & to extrapolate the significance of them. Student can trace and evaluate arguments or specific claims in the texts and assess their effectiveness. Student chooses clear, strong, and relevant evidence and clearly connects it to their analysis.
	Organization Standards: 8.W.1c, 1e, 2c, 2f, 4; 7	The essay has no clear structure or transitions between ideas.	Student includes an introduction, body, and conclusion in the essay but doesn't write complete paragraphs or sentences. The introduction may not include a claim while the conclusion may only consist of a generalities or filler sentences.	Student includes an introduction, body, and conclusion in the essay. The introduction includes a claim while the conclusion attempts to wrap up the essay by simply rephrasing or repeating the claim. Student attempts to use transition words, phrases, or clauses but essay might still feel choppy.	Student includes a clear introduction, body, and conclusion in the essay. The introduction includes an interesting hook and clear claim while the conclusion neatly wraps up and supports the essay. Student uses transition words, phrases, or clauses to create a cohesive argument.	Student includes a clear introduction, body, and conclusion in the essay. The introduction includes an interesting hook and clear, concise claim while the conclusion neatly wraps up and supports the essay while adding a new and insightful way to look at the claim. Student creatively uses vivid and interesting transition words, phrases, or clauses to create a fluid, cohesive argument.

x1	Language Standards: 8.RI/RL.4; 7.W.1d, 2d, 2e; 8.L.1-5	Student's text is barely legible due to many grammar and spelling mistakes. Student fails to maintain a formal style.	Student has several grammar or spelling mistakes. Student attempts a formal style but still has several slang terms or personal pronouns.	Student uses correct grammar and spelling. Student mostly maintains a formal style throughout the text removing most slang and personal pronouns but might have missed a few.	Student uses correct grammar and spelling, choosing appropriate, interesting language (including any technical terminology from the text) to add variety to the text. Student maintains a formal style throughout the text, removing all slang and personal pronouns.	Student uses correct grammar and spelling. Student chooses appropriate, interesting language (including any technical terminology from the text) & factors in connotation & context in order to add variety, precision, & conciseness to the text. Student maintains a formal style throughout the text, removing all slang and personal pronouns.

For when students share research in a class discussion

x1	Preparation and Collaboration Standards: 8.SL.1a-d	Students do not come to discussions or the presentation prepared. The group squabbles and cannot get along or work together.	Some students come to group discussions and/or the presentation prepared, having read most materials and/or completing assigned tasks. Students attempt open discussion, but several discussions are heated or ineffective. Students struggle to acknowledge new information or ideas expressed by others and/or struggle to find acceptable compromises. Students struggle to ask questions and/or answer questions posed by others. Students do not attempt to track progress and fall behind in their project.	Most students come to group discussions prepared for the presentation, having read all materials and/or completed assigned tasks. Students are open to discussion but there are a few ineffective discussions. Students acknowledge new information or ideas expressed by others and are able to compromise though some students may still feel left out. Students are able to pose questions & answer them from others. Students attempt to track progress but may miss specific deadlines or may not accomplish all goals.	All students come to all group discussions and the presentation prepared, having read all materials and/or completing assigned tasks. Students are open to discussion but there might be some easily resolved though heated discussions. Students acknowledge new information or ideas expressed by others and are able to form acceptable compromises. Students are able to pose questions and answer questions posed by others. Students track progress and keep specific goals and deadlines.	All students come to all group discussions and the presentation prepared, having read all materials and/or completing assigned tasks. Students are open to reasonable discussions without arguments. Students acknowledge new information or ideas expressed by others are able to create solutions/ideas that work for all. Students are able to pose thought-provoking questions and insightfully answer questions posed by others. Students effectively track progress and keep specific goals and deadlines.

For when students present research as a group in front of the class

x1	Presentation and Articulation Standards: 8.SL.4, 6; 8.L.3	Most or all of the students' claims and ideas are confusing. Most students are off task & unfocused. Students do not make good eye contact/or use an appropriate volume. There are many pronunciation errors and students sound monotone. There is no obvious organization, and no one knows who is supposed to speak.	Some of the students' claims and ideas are confusing. Several students are off task and unfocused. Students struggle to make good eye contact and/or use an appropriate volume. There are many pronunciation errors and students struggle to vary their tone. The presentation is poorly organized and/or the students do not know who is supposed to speak.	Students present their claims, findings, and ideas mostly coherently. Most students are on task and focused. Most students make good eye contact and use an appropriate volume. There are few pronunciation errors and students attempt to vary their tone in order to emphasize their important points. The presentation is mostly organized.	Students present their claims, findings, and ideas coherently. No student it off task or unfocused. Students make strong eye contact and use an appropriate volume. All words are clearly pronounced, and students vary their tone in order to emphasize salient points. The presentation is well organized.	Students present their claims, findings, and ideas coherently and engagingly. No student it off task or unfocused. All students make strong eye contact and use an appropriate volume that can be heard from anywhere in the room. All words are clearly and correctly pronounced, and students vary their tone and speech appropriately for the style of presentation in order to emphasize salient points and/or to create excitement/engagement with their listeners. Presentation is smooth and well organized.

Appendix B
Additional Sources

Duane A. Cline, *The Pilgrims and Plymouth Colony: 1620*, 1999.
  http://sites.rootsweb.com/~mosmd/index.htm#part2

This site has an incredible amount of information for teachers and students, not just on the Pilgrims and Plymouth Colony, but also on sailing and navigational tools. He includes numerous student activities for creating and using the navigational tools of the 17th century. These include creating:

- Sandglasses
- Mariner's Magnetic Compass
- The Back-Staff
- The Astrolabe
- The Nocturnal
- The Mariner's Quadrant
- The Traverse Board
- The Compass Rose
- The Log-Line
- The Hand Lead-Line
- The Cross Staff

Smithsonian, "Time and Navigation: The Untold Story of Getting from Here to There"
  https://timeandnavigation.si.edu

This site has a lot of information for students and teachers, including navigating at sea, in the air and in space, satellite navigation, a timeline of innovation, and videos explaining how latitude and longitude and GPS work.

Vanderhoof Family History Project
  http://www.vanderhoofproject.com/index.php/the-journey/more-about-de-bever

This site has the original Journal of De Bever, 1661 both in Dutch and English along with passenger lists, including the amounts of money owed by those who indentured themselves to take the voyage, letters from the WIC Directors to Peter Stuyvesant, maps, and other genealogical information.

Elford Eddy, **The Log of a Cabin Boy**, 1922
>   https://books.google.com/books?id=Jug7AQAAMAAJ&printsec=frontcover&source=gbs_ge_summary_r&cad=0#v=onepage&q&f=false

>   This book is available as a free ebook on Google Books and can be downloaded as a pdf.

Richard's Dystopian Pokeverse, "Dutch Ships in the 17th Century: a diorama for CCH"
>   https://lurkerablog.wordpress.com/2013/12/09/dutch-ships-in-the-17th-century-a-diorama-for-cch/

>   This website contains information on Texel Harbor in the Netherlands, along with maps and beautiful images of dioramas showing what the harbor would have looked like in the 17th century. He also includes maps and images of Amsterdam.

Marcus Flynn, **Pyromasse**, "Les Potagers"
>   https://www.pyromasse.ca/articles/potager_e.html

>   This website provides information and many photographs and diagrams of the 17th century French stoves discussed in *Thrown to the Wind*.

Appendix C
Sources Cited for *A Home in the Wilderness*

Images and Illustrations

Included in *A Home in the Wilderness* (in order of appearance)

Moran, Edward (1829-1901). *Henrick Hudson Entering New York Harbor*, September 11, 1609. Berkshire Museum, Public Domain.

Visscher II, Nicolaes (1649-1702). *New Netherland Map.* Media file donated from Koninklijke Bibliotheek, Public Domain.

Manhattan Island, 1639. Library of Congress, Public Domain.

Detail *Manhattan Island*, 1639. Library of Congress, Public Domain.

Redraft of the Castillo Plan, New Amsterdam, 1660. Wikimedia Commons. Public Domain.

Ricker, James. "New Harlem Village Plot, 1670," *Revised History of Harlem (New York City): Its Origin and Early Annals ...*, page 291, 1904. (See full citation below.)

Weir, Robert Walter (1803-1889). *Landing of Henry Hudson*, 1609, at Verplanck Point, New York. Public Domain.

Tantillo, L.F. Painting of *1695 Kingston.* Senate House Historic Site, Kingston, NY, Office of Parks, Recreation and Historic Preservation, 2015.

Nichol, Spencer. *The Town of Pomeiock*, Library of Congress. Public Domain.

Family Histories and Genealogies

Dayton, Edson C. *The Record of a Family Decent from Ralph Dayton and Alice (Goldhatch) Tritton, Married June 16, 1617, Ashford, County Kent, England: A Genealogical and Biographical Account of One Branch of the Dayton Family in America.* Caroline K. Dayton, 1931.

Griffin, Judy. *Gano Family*, 2007.

Gunnoe, Judith. *The Gunnoe Family of West Virginia*, 5/25/2013.

Hervey, Robert. "Early Gano History," *Hervey Family History, 2001.* Lineage Online.

Jacobus, Donald Lines, and Arthur Bliss Dayton. *The Early Daytons and Descendants of Henry, Jr.* New Haven, CT: New Haven Colony Historical Society, 1959.

Lemaster, Howard Marshall. *Gano Family, U.S.A., 1970.* Carlinville, IL, 1970.

Native Americans

Barron, Donna Gentle Spirit, *The Long Island Indians And Their New England Ancestors: Narragansett, Mohegan, Pequot, & Wampanoag Tribes.* Bloomington, IN: AuthorHouse, 2006. Print.

Bierhorst, John, Ed. *The White Deer and Other Stories Told by the Lenape.* New York: William Morrow and Company, Inc., 1995.

From this source, I used several quotes and retellings of some of these myths.

Calloway, Colin G. *First Peoples: A Documentary Survey of American Indian History, 5th Edition.* Boston & New York: Bedford/St. Martin's, 2016.

Cohen, Doris Darlington. "The Weckquaesgeek." Ardsley Historical Society. N.D. Web.

This was a valuable source for specific information on the Native American tribe living on Manhattan and the southeastern side of the Hudson River.

Curry, Jane Louise. *Turtle Island: Tales of the Algonquian Nations.* New York, NY: Margaret K. McElderry Books, 1999. Print.

From this source, I used quotes and retellings of some of these myths.

Hitakonanu'laxk (Tree Beard). *The Grandfathers Speak: Native American Folk Tales of the Lenapé People.* New York: Interlink Books, 2012. Print.

From this source, I used quotes and retellings of some of these myths.

Lipman, Andrew. *The Saltwater Frontier: Indians and the Contest for the American Coast.* New Haven and London: Yale University Press, 2015. Print.

This was an invaluable source in giving the history of the Native Americans, Europeans, and their interactions prior to the European arrival through 1750. It details the politics, economies, society, cultures, and interactions between the various tribes of the region, their vessels and those of the Europeans, and interactions between the various European and Native groups.

Matthews, Christopher N., and Allison Manfra McGovern. "Created Communities: Segregation and the History of Plural Sites on Eastern Long Island, New York," *Society for Historical Archaeology,* 2018.

Maynard, Eric (Mohegan). "American Indian Film Gallery," AIFG, 2013. Accessed March 2, 2019. Web.

Sleeper-Smith, Susan, Ed. *Rethinking the Fur Trade: Cultures of Exchange in an Atlantic World.* Lincoln & London: University of Nebraska Press, 2009. Print.

Strong, John A. *The Montaukett Indians of Eastern Long Island.* Syracuse, NY: Syracuse University Press, 2001. Print.

Thomas, R. Murray. *Manitou and God: North American Indian Religions and Christian Culture.* Westport, CT: Praeger Publishers, an imprint of Greenwood Publishing Group, Inc., 2007.

This source was invaluable in helping me understand the fundamental beliefs of the Algonquian people and comparing the differences and similarities between the native religion and Christianity.

Turner, Timothy. Wampanoag Homesite Blog and Videos, including "Wampanoag Man Working on a Boat," "Cooking in a Clay Pot," "Mashoon (Canoe) Finished," "Tour of Wampanoag Homesite," *Plimoth Plantation Museum.* Accessed October 25, 2019. Web.

> This site was invaluable in providing visual demonstrations of how the Eastern Woodland people lived with explanations in some cases of why they did certain things the way they did. It was nice to see the Native Americans showing how they had carried down their traditions through the generations.

Unknown director (possibly Crawley, Frank Randford "Budge"). Unknown writer. *How Indians Build Canoes.* Crawley Films, 1946. Film.

> Another excellent video documentation that showed how Native Americans made birch bark canoes.

New York (New Netherlands) Colony

"Appendix J: Cultural Resource Maps," *DEIS*, DME Projects. New York City: Historical Perspectives, Inc., n.d. Available on the NYC.gov website.

Cohen, Paul E., and Robert T. Augustyn. *Manhattan in Maps: 1527-1995.* New York, New York: Rizzoli International Publications, Inc., 1997. Web.

> In addition to providing a large number of historic maps of Manhattan, this book also provides a thorough history of Manhattan from early colonization to the twentieth century.

Dietz, Theodore. *Dutch Esopus/Wiltwyck/Kingston Memories.* Pittsburgh, Pennsylvania: Dorrance Publishing Co., Inc., 2012. Print.

> This book was valuable in providing descriptions of the village and region of the Esopus and Wiltwyck and confirming some of the histories of the area.

Elson, Henry William, and Kathy Leigh, translator. "New Amsterdam," *History of the United States.* New York: MacMillan Company, 1904. Web.

> This well-footnoted history of the colony of New Amsterdam is a good general history of the colony.

Fried, Marc B. *The Early History of Kingston & Ulster Country, N.Y.* Marbletown, Kingston, NY: Ulster County Historical Society, 1975.

Gardiner, Jonathan T., Jonathan Baker, Joseph S. Osborn, Eds. *Records of the Town of East-Hampton, Long Island, Suffolk Co., N.Y., with Other Ancient Documents of Historic Value.*, Vol. 1. SAG-Harbor, N.Y.: John H. Hunt, Printer, 1887.

Jacobs, Jaap, *The Colony of New Netherland: A Dutch Settlement in Seventeenth-Century America.* Ithaca, NY: Cornell University, 2009. Print.

Kregier, Capt. Martin, *Journal of the Second Esopus War: With an account of the Massacre at Wildwyck, the names of those killed, wounded, and taken prisoners by the Indians on that occasion, 1663.* Translated from the original Dutch MS. Provided by Ed St. Germain and available at www.americanrevolution.org.

This source was invaluable in retracing the Dutch reponse to the Esopus attack at Wiltwyck.

Leng, Charles W., B.Sc. and William T. Davis. *Staten Island and Its People: A History 1609 – 1929,* Vols. 1-2, New York, NY: Lewis Historical Publishing Company, Inc., 1930.

Matteo, Thomas. "Staten Island Brief History," *The Staten Island Historian.* Staten Island, NY: Rhinostudio.com, 2008-2012. Web.

Ricker, James. *Revised History of Harlem (City of New York): Its gin and Early Annals: Prefaced by Homes Scenes in the Fatherlands; Or Notices of Its Founders Before Emigration. Also, Sketches of Numerous Families, and the Recovered History of the Land-Titles....* New York, NY: New Harlem Publishing Company, 1904.

Shorto, Russell, *The Island at the Center of the World: The Epic Story of Dutch Manhattan and the Forgotten Colony that Shaped America,* NY: Vintage Books, Division of Random House, Inc., 2004. Print.

This source contained invaluable information on all sorts of information on the communities, maritime activities, trade relations, and in answering numerous other questions.

Staten Island Advance. *History: A Timeline of Staten Island.* SILive.com, 2014. Web.

Steinmeyer, Henry G. *Staten Island 1524 – 1898.* Richmondtown, Staten Island, N.Y.: The Staten Island Historical Society, 1959.

"Street Plan of New Amsterdam and Colonial New York," *Landmarks Preservation Commission,* June 14. 1983, Designation List 165 LP-1235.

Sublett, John, Louis. *Staten Island Folklore.* Amazon Digital Services, Inc., June 1, 2011. Kindle Book.

Sublett, John Louis. *Staten Island: A Walk Down Memory Lane.* CreateSpace, January 28, 2009. Kindle Book.

This book provides a convenient timeline of significant events affecting Staten Island and some information on the island's prominent people. It also provides a valuable listing of books on Staten Island.

Tantillo, L.F. Painting of *1695 Kingston.* Senate House Historic Site, Kingston, NY, Office of Parks, Recreation and Historic Preservation, 2015.

I used this image to visualize and describe the settlement of Wiltwyck and the surrounding landscape.

Tantillo, L.F. *A Moment Past: L. F. Tantillo Paints New York History.* Nassau, NY: L.F. Tantillo, Fine Art, 2014. Print.

Tantillo, L.F. *The Edge of New Netherland.* Nassau, NY: L.F. Tantillo, Fine Art, 2011. Print.

Vail, Emily. "History: Colonization," *Tracing the Tannery Brook Project.* Cornell University, NYS Water Resources Institute; NYS Department of Environmental Conservation, Hudson River Estuary Program; NYS Environmental Protection Fund. Web.

This site was valuable in supplying descriptions, images, and maps of historic Wiltwyck.

Whitehouse, Jack. *Fire Island: Heroes & Villains on Long Island's Wild Shore.* Charleston, SC: The History Press, 2011. Print.

The stories in this book helped paint a picture of what life was like on Long Island. It also provided more information on the "royal fishes," or drift whales, that were claimed by the governors of Long Island but whose laws the colonists resisted.

Additional Sources for Teacher's Resource
Alligood, Nekole. "The History of the Delaware Nation," *Delaware Nation.* Web. Accessed 4/9/2024.

Andrew Evans. "Traveling to the End of the World," *National Geographic*, February 9, 2012. Accessed September 7, 2024.

Benchley, Nathaniel. *"The $24 Swindle,"* *American Heritage Magazine*, December 1959. Accessed March 14, 2024.

Brodhead, John Romeyn, et. Al. "Miller Map of Kingston Stockade Area in 1695 as Designated by Governor Petrus Stuyvesant." *Documents Relative to the Colonial History of the State of New-York: Procured in Holland, England, and France*, Vol. XIII, Albany: Weed, Parsons, 1853. Ulster County Archives.

Cohen, Doris Darlington. "The Weckquaesgeek," with verbal guidance from Nicholas Shoumatoff, Curator and Delaware Expert at Ward Pound Trailside Museum and his library, n.d.

Coolman, Robert and Owen Jarus, "Keeping Time: The origin of B.C. and A.D.", January 14, 2022. Accessed September 9, 2024.

Craddock, Bob. "The Science of Leap Year," *National Air and Space Museum.* Smithsonian. February 27, 2020. Accessed September 10, 2024.

Egloff, Nancy D. "The Tragedy of 1622: The Powhatan Paramount Chiefdom Military Offensive Against English Settlers in Virginia," Jamestown-Yorktown Foundation, n.d.

Egyptian Obelisk, Image taken by Ahmed M. Hanfy, April 14, 2018. Creative Commons Attribution-Share Alike 4.0 International.

Fried, Marc B. Fried. *The Early History of Kingston & Ulster County, NY.* Marbletown, Kingston, NY: Ulster County Historical Society, 1975.

Goddard, Ives (2010). *"The Origin and Meaning of the Name "Manhattan"*. New York History. **91** (4): 277–293. hdl:10088/16790. ISSN 0146-437X – via Smithsonian Research Online.

"Heavenly Stems and Earthly Branches," *Hong Kong Observatory.* Accessed September 9, 2024.

History.com Editors. *"New Amsterdam becomes New York,"* *History*, A&E Television Networks. May 19, 2023. Retrieved March 15, 2024.

Howe, Richard. "Notes On The Manhattan Purchase," The Gotham Center for New York City History. June 27, 2012. Accessed March 14, 2024.

Jacobs, Jaap. *The Colony of New Netherland: A Dutch Settlement in Sevententh-Century America.* Ithaca, NY: Cornwell University, 2009.

Janos.NYC, *"Today in NYC History: How the Dutch Actually Bought Manhattan (The Long Version),"* *Today in NYC History.* N.d. Accessed March 14, 2024.

Juet, Robert (2006) [1625]. "Juet's Journal of Hudson's 1609 Voyage, from the 1625 Edition of *Purchas His Pilgrimes*". *The New York Times.* Translated by Brea Barthel. p. 16. Archived from the original on July 3, 2016. Retrieved May 11, 2020.

Kregier, Capt. Martin. *Journal of the Second Esopus War: With an account of the Massacre at Wiltwyck, the names of those killed, wounded, and taken prisoners, by the Indians of that occasion, 1663.* Translated from the original Dutch MS.

Levine, David. *Hudson Valley,* "The Esopus Wars: A History of the Battle Between the Dutch and Local American Indians in the 1660s," 10/23/2013. Accessed 5/10/2020.

Mashantucket Pequot Museum & Research Center "Causes of the Pequot War,", n.d. Accessed July 22, 2024.

Miller, Robert J. "Economic Development in Indian Country: Will Capitalism or Socialism Succeed?" Oregon Law Review, Vol. 80, No. 3, Fall 2001.

Newman, John, Geshe Lhundub Sopa (ed.). *The Wheel of Time: Kalachakra in Context.* Shambhala, 1991.

"Of Plymouth Plantation: Early American Digital Archive (EADA)." Archived from the original on 2018-06-25. Retrieved July 22, 2024.

"Pequot War – Connecticut History: A CT Humanities Project," n.d.

"Projections of the shadow of the Sun, at noon, at the solstices, in Luxor," diagram by Aubry Gérard. Creative Commons Attribution-Share Alike 4.0 License.

Replica of a Roman sundial (scaphe), by Manfred Heyde, September 2008. Public Domain.

Steele, John M. ed. "The Chinese Sexagenary Cycle and Ritual Origins of the Calendar," in *Calendars and Years II: Astronomy and Time in the Ancient and Medieval World.* Oxford: Oxbow Books, 2010.

"The Calendar System," *Living Maya Time*. The Smithsonian National Museum of the American Indians. Accessed September 9, 2024.

"The Sinnington sundial," photo by Pauline E. Creative Commons Attribution-Share Alike 2.0.

White, W.E. "The Anglo-Powhatan War of 1622," Christopher Newport University, n.d.